The Mythology of the Mermaid and Her Kin

Marc Potts

www.capallbann.co.uk

The Mythology of the Mermaid and Her Kin

©2000 Marc Potts

ISBN 186163 0395

Cover design by Paul Mason
Cover and internal illustrations by Marc Potts

Published by:

Capall Bann Publishing
Freshfields
Chieveley
Berks
RG20 8TF

Dedication

Dedicated to my partner Lynn, for her belief and her support
and to my daughter Carys, my own Little Mermaid

This book is also dedicated to the Great Goddess of the Sea.
Long may she swim the oceans of the world.

Contents

Introduction

Ever since man first gazed out over the open ocean, his fascination with it has been complete.

In total awe of its mighty destructive power, its majestic beauty and its mysterious depths, man has always populated the ocean with the fabulous and the bizarre. Sea farers would tell tales of amazing sea-creatures; immense fish that spouted water and steam, great sea-serpents that could destroy a ship in moments and many-armed monsters that could pluck an unwary sailor from the very deck.

Amongst the fantastic creatures encountered by sea farers were, arguably, the most unlikely of all. These were the mer-folk, the fish-tailed women and men and their equally unlikely kin. Central to the legends of these half fish, half human beings was the mermaid. From the primeval waters at the beginning of time to the oceans of today, she remains more or less unchanged.

There are three main ways to approach the study of the mer-folk and other water-spirits. The first is by their folklore and mythology. The second is the approach of zoology, or rather 'cryptozoology', the study of hidden (or misinterpreted?), nature. The third approach is that of water-spirit as a purely elemental being, representing water itself. This book is primarily concerned with the first approach, but I have included a short chapter on mermaid sightings and captures. As to the third approach, there are many excellent books on the subject of elemental magic and I leave this one to them.

The mermaid is as complex as she is improbable. On one hand she is as treacherous and deadly as she is beautiful. Unlucky indeed was the poor doomed soul that heard her siren song.

Mere mortal man was helpless before the seductive powers of the 'femme fatale' of the sea.

This is, however, only one point of view, perpetuated mainly since the advent of Christianity. To the early Christian Church the image of the 'pagan' mermaid served as a warning. She represented the dangers of female licentiousness, the wanton and destructive nature of a pagan goddess.

The mermaid of European folklore, the 'creature' I am primarily concerned with in this book, was not totally preoccupied with luring unwary sailors and fishermen to a watery grave, or some other-worldly marriage. She had gentler traits as well, and her folklore bears this out. All too often, the mermaid was the victim of man, and if she chose to cause him problems, it was often in retribution for a wrong done to her or her kind.

The story of the mermaid is deep-rooted and powerful, but her nature has changed a little along the way, even if her basic appearance has not. From fish-tailed goddess she has become the hopelessly doomed and wretched pagan creature that longed for salvation in a Christian heaven. The mythology of the mer-folk and their kin stretches back into the mists of antiquity. They appear in the mythologies of cultures from all over the world. It would seem that wherever man has had contact with the sea, he has had to deal with sea-spirits that were part human and part sea-beast, and more often than not, part fish. The mermaid is as much at home in the open waters of the Pacific as she is off the rocky coasts of Cornwall or Shetland. Sometimes she even appears in lakes, pools or wells!

So where does she come from? It is true that there are many tales of her mate, the merman, but many cultures associated the seas and oceans with the feminine. Many ancient sea-goddesses and sea-gods resemble the modern day image of the mermaid and merman.

Sir Thomas Browne (1605-1682), writing in Elizabethan times considered the myth of the mer-folk to have sprung from memories of ancient sea deities. The mer-folk were the descendants of pagan gods and goddesses such as..

"Dagon, Atergatis or Derceto, from whence were probably occasioned the pictures of Nereides and Tritons among the Grecians"

The ancient sea deities are most certainly the illustrious ancestors of the mer-folk and this will be explored in chapter 2.

From this point the mermaid will be traced, via her folklore up to the present day. Along the way I will examine encounters with and reports of mermaids, her curious relationship with the early Christian Church, and her representations in art, literature and poetry.

Few people today would not be familiar with the image of the mermaid. Her general appearance and characteristics are well defined. At the beginning of this brief introduction I described the mermaid as a 'femme fatale' avid for the lives of men. It would be unfair to ignore her kindly aspects, and I also indicated that she has a gentler side. I will start by presenting aspects of the mermaid's character, both sides of the coin, as it were.

This book is by no means a definitive work on the mermaid, merely an introduction to her, her kin and their mythology. This is my version of the mermaid's tale.

Goddess of the Sea

Chapter 1

The Mermaid's Tale:
Her Appearance and
Character

The mermaid sits amongst the rocks at the edge of the sea and presses a golden comb to the end of her long auburn tresses. Behind her small waves break gently, hissing their own song, urging her to return to them. She has an other-worldly beauty, but her expression is wistful, even sad. Her eyes betray dreams of a secret longing and her softly parted lips yearn for the forbidden kiss that can never be hers.

Above the waist her skin is smooth, pale and perfect, but below are the shimmering, silver scales of a fish. The mermaid's tail is coiled around her body and before her an iridescent shell is full of pearls with which she will stud her hair.

In 1833 six fishermen from the Shetland island of Yell discovered a bizarre creature entangled in their nets. The men pulled the creature aboard and kept it for three hours. In this way they were able to give a good account of its appearance.

The creature was about three feet in length, the upper part resembling woman, but with a face more likened to that of a monkey. The creature had short arms, which she kept crossed over human-like breasts as if acutely embarrassed. Below the waist was a tail, similar, according to the fishermen, to that of a dogfish. No gills or fins were evident, but there was a crest of bristles on the head and neck that could be raised and lowered at will. The creature was without both scales or hair.

During the three hours, the creature offered no resistance to her captors, but lay in the boat moaning pitifully. This, combined with their superstition, eventually got the better of the fishermen and they released the creature unharmed. The creature disappeared into the depths and was not seen again.

Descriptions of two very different creatures, but both are descriptions of mermaids. The first is of a beautiful fish-tailed woman sitting on rocks, combing her long hair with a golden comb. This is the classical image of the mermaid; the picture conjured in the minds of most people by the term. It is a description of the mermaid of folklore, the romantic creature perpetuated by artists and poets down through the ages.

In fact the description in the first passage is that of a painting entitled 'A Mermaid' by the great Romantic Classicist painter John William Waterhouse. Waterhouse painted 'A Mermaid', in typical Pre-Raphaelite style, in 1901 for an exhibition at the Royal Academy. It is one of his most beautiful and delicate compositions, and is perfectly evocative of the mermaid as people imagine her today.

The second passage is based on an account that first appeared in Dr. Robert Hamilton's *History of Whales and Seals* published in 1839. The story had been related to Dr. Hamilton, the Professor of Natural History at Edinburgh University, by a Mr Edmonston. Mr Edmonston had got the account himself directly from the skipper of the fishing boat. Mr Edmonston had stated that the skipper had no doubt in his mind that the creature he and his men had captured had been a mermaid. Although the fishermen had kept the 'mermaid' for three hours, they had certainly done her no harm. Every man of those parts knew that to do so would have brought much misfortune. Such was the belief in mermaids in those days.

'The Mermaid of Yell' hardly fits the classical image of the 'maid of the sea', but it demonstrates that firm belief in her existed, in places where her tradition is strongest, in the last century. That tradition and belief almost certainly lingers today.

So, to return to the more familiar mermaid image, what exactly are those well defined characteristics mentioned in the introduction?

Robert Graves wrote; "The mermaid stands for the bitter-sweetness of love and for the danger run by susceptible mariners in foreign ports". Her traditional mirror and comb stand for vanity and heartlessness. A woman beyond all mortal beauty from the waist up, with a fish's tail below; she is the love-goddess risen from the sea, Aphrodite in her mermaid form. And with the 'morals' of a Pagan love-goddess, the mermaid represented the sin of forbidden love and the wantonness of woman-kind to the early Christian Church.

Traditionally then, the mermaid of European folklore has long flowing hair, and where descriptions are given, it is usually blond or black in colour. The mermaids of the Faeroe Islands are said to have long brown hair which floats about them as they swim, Those in Irish waters are sometimes said to have silver tresses. But, as if to give emphasis to their other-worldly nature, the mermaid and more especially the merman are also described with green hair. The Irish mer-folk are the merrows, and in the tale of 'Blind Maurice', told later, the eponymous hero is lured to the sea by the singing of "an unnatural thing in the form of a green-haired lady". Although the female merrows are beautiful, with their long flowing hair, white skin and dark eyes, the males are very ugly creatures. The male merrows have not only green hair, but green teeth and skin. Their eyes are small, deep-set and piggy and their noses long and red. For all their ugliness however, the male merrow is usually a jovial and friendly creature.

Another benign merman with green (or black) hair and beard, is the havmand of Norway. The havmand differs from his Irish counterpart however, as he is described as a handsome creature. The havfrue is the mermaid of Norway, and in direct opposition to her mate is usually thought of as treacherous and evil.

The beauty of the mermaid is accentuated by her pale, sometimes snow white skin. An early Irish legend tells of an encounter with mermaids by the hero Rath. The mermaids had the shape of the fairest of girls with yellow hair and white skins. Another tale from Irish mythology describes a gigantic mermaid, one hundred and ninety-five feet long, whiter than a swan all over. According to J.A. Macculloch in *Myths of all Races: Celtic* (1918), this huge creature was washed ashore in the country of Alba.

A bestiary published in 1599 and written by the naturalist Ulysses Aldovardi describes a mermaid and merman seen in the River Nile. The *Historic Monstrorum* describes the female as white skinned with black hair. The male, on the other hand, had brown skin, red hair and "a terrible aspect".

Mermaids were a fact of maritime life in the Channel Islands, where they were more commonly known by the French term 'Sirens', (Les Sirenes). Although the sirens of Sark were traditionally young-looking and beautiful, fishermen in Guernsey described their mermaids as old women with fish's tails. Both types nevertheless were considered equally dangerous, singing before storms that would dash a ship to pieces. The mermaids of the Channel Islands would lay in wait and drag down any sailor they found floundering after the wreck. Once captured, the unfortunate sailors were devoured.

An integral part of the mermaid is her fish's tail. The Ben-Varrey (bedn varra) is the Manx mermaid, and with her mate the Dooiney Marrey (dunya mara), is described as having "...the lower parts of a fish, complete with fins and huge spreading tail".

In the folk-tale *John Reid and the Mermaid* the mermaid in question has a long silvery tail, which she presses against a rock until it curls up to her waist. In this fashion the mermaid then thrusts forward and pushes herself into the sea.

The Ceasg (keeask) of Highland folklore is a mermaid with the upper body of a beautiful woman and, below the waist, the tail of a grisle (a young salmon). The mermaid of the Irish legend *Liban* also has a salmon's tail.

Aside from folklore and legend, a mermaid was reported from Benbecula in the 1830's by local people who were cutting seaweed. She was described as childlike in proportion from the waist up, but with the tail of a salmon below. Although the 'human' part of the mermaid was about the size of a three or four year old, she had the developed breasts of an adult. Her hair was dark and glossy, and her skin white and soft. This detailed description was possible, as the poor creature had been washed up dead and found by seaweed cutters. As testimony to the 'humaness' of this particular mermaid, the locals made her a small coffin and buried her on the shore.

Other mermaids are given the tails of porpoises and dolphins. Some have been described as eel-like. A mermaid, apparently drawn from life, appeared in a work on marine natural history in 1717. The book had an unwieldy title: *Poissons, ecrevisses et crabes de diverse coleurs et figures extraordinaire, que l'on trouve autour des Isles Moluques*. The 'Mermaid of Amboine', as the creature was known, had a tail "..in proportion as an eel". Delicate pink hairs ran the length of the tail and the skin of the mermaid had an olive tint. The picture in the book shows the creature perfectly human from the waist up.

The Tritons of Ancient Greece were described by Pausanius in book IX of *Descriptions of Greece* (translated by W.H.S. Jones in 1918). According to this learned man they had dolphin-like tails under the breast and belly instead of feet. In Indonesian legend a mermaid type creature called a Rujung was woman above the waist, but dolphin below. The Rujung eventually transforms wholly into a dolphin (having initially been a normal woman). From the realms of cryptozoology comes the 1984 report in the *Weekly World News* that reported the attempted seduction of an Amazonian fisherman by a mermaid with the tail of a porpoise. Japanese mythology describes the Samebito, a merman that has a shark's tail. Another Japanese mermaid, the Mu Jima, has small forelegs and is covered with hair.

Occasionally the mermaid is depicted as a twin-tailed creature. This is not the mermaid of folklore, but rather an image sometimes found in church carvings and, more commonly, in heraldry. Examples exist at Chanteuges and Brioude in the Auvergne. At Brioude, carved stone mermaids face mermen across the nave. The twin tails of both seem to end in foliage-like fins, suggesting a crossover between the mermaid and 'green man' imagery so often found in European churches.

Further north at Sealand, Vigersted church has a 15th century wall painting showing a twin-tailed mermaid holding two long plaits of her own hair in each hand. St.Peter's church in Cambridge has a twin-tailed merman encircling the font. Merfolk with two tails are also found outside churches. An example from heraldry is found on the coat of arms granted to Samuel of Manchester in 1958. Much further back in time, a twin-tailed mermaid has been identified carved on a stone of Pictish origin. This stone is one of the carved 'Meigle Stones' housed at the Meigle museum in Perthshire. Interestingly, the carving shows the mermaid grasping her plaited hair as with the Vigersted example. Both were probably influenced by drawings in early bestiaries.

The Picts are generally accepted to have had water cults, salmon and dolphin were sacred animals and were frequently carved. Other Pictish carvings feature one of the oldest pieces of goddess symbolism of all; the mirror and the comb, and what mermaid is complete without a golden comb with which to untangle her long hair and a shell encrusted mirror in which to admire the results.

Of course, the comb and mirror are another integral part of mermaid mythology; at least they are in keeping with her most popular conception. Robert Graves has theorised that the comb may have originally been a plectrum for playing the lyre. The plectrum changed to a comb due to artistic misinterpretation and the latter became a valid symbol of the goddess in its own right.

Graves suggests that the mirror may represent the moon. A reflection of this is that there is often a link and a certain degree of crossover, between moon and sea goddesses. Water is the original mirror, reflecting the moon above as it moves over the dark sea. The mirror was sacred to the Eleusinian Mysteries, which were of Pelasgian origin. The Pelasgians were an indigenous people of Ancient Greece, whose name means 'sea-farers', and they claimed descent from the mermaid goddess Eurynome.

Returning to the mermaid, of European folklore at least, she is often found with comb and mirror. The comb is not just for beautification, it is important. To acquire it gives power over the mermaid. In the Cornish tale *Lutey and the Mermaid* the Cornishman of the title is given a golden comb with a pearl handle in return for saving the mermaid's life. She tells Lutey to pass the comb three times through the water whenever he is in need and she would come to his aid. Lutey's tale is told in full later.

In a tale from the Isle of Skye a man manages to creep up to a mermaid that is laying with the baby seals. The mermaid herself is too quick for the man and escapes, but one of the baby seals is not so lucky and is grabbed by the man. The mermaid soon reappears, with others of her kind, and demands that the man release the seal. The man tries to bargain and says that he will release the seal if the mermaid gives him her comb.

Knowing that if she does this the man will forever have power over her she, not surprisingly, refuses. The man settles for three wishes and the seal is released.

The mermaid is often depicted with mirror and comb in church carvings. The famous 'mermaid seat' still exists in Zennor church, the bench end, carved in the 15th century, shows her holding both. Many other examples exist.

A close relative of the mermaid are the 'wasser nixen' (water sprites) or nixes. They are often described as beautiful women that loved to sit and admire their reflections as they combed their long hair. The same is said of the Lorelei, the female water spirits of the River Rhine.

In Irish and Scottish folklore the mermaid was also found with another important item. This was either a magic cap or feather in Ireland, or a magic belt in Scotland (and sometimes England). The Irish mer-folk, or merrows used a magic cap, the 'cohuleen druith', to propel themselves under water. The cap was usually red in colour (as was the feather if used for the same purpose), and if it was ever lost the merrow could not return to the sea. Mortal men sometimes secured for themselves mermaid brides by stealing the *cohuleen druith*, and effectively holding the mermaid to ransom. This very common theme is found throughout mermaid folklore.

In a tale from Ireland a male merrow, that has befriended a young man, willingly lends him his *cohuleen druith*, (a spare one), and takes him to visit his undersea realm.

In the Hebrides particularly, and elsewhere in Scotland, a magic belt shares the same properties as the *cohuleen druith*. Likewise, without the belt the mermaid or merman is trapped on land and powerless to return to the sea.

And what of the mermaid's nature? European folklore tends to treat her as a dangerous temptress, luring seafarers to their deaths. Her singing voice is that of the siren, driving mad all those who hear it, or else it is captivating and enchanting in its seductive power. We must start with the song of the mermaid, the song of the primeval sea itself.

In Cornwall to hear a mermaid's song was often the fore-warning of a storm. Near Lamorna Cove in the far west of that county is The Mermaid's Rock. A mermaid would sing from the rock and to the local people this was a sure sign of bad weather at sea, and the wreck of a ship was inevitable. Already mentioned is the mermaid of Zennor. This is an interesting reversal of the mermaid luring a man to the sea with her song. In the tale the mermaid is enchanted by the beautiful singing of a local choir boy and falls in love with him.

The song of the mermaid is duly noted in the medieval bestiaries. The work of Guillaume le clerc, written in 1210-1211, was in the form of old Norman rhyme, and translated into English in 1936 by George Claridge Druce. In a section on the siren, Guillaume describes her sweet singing voice, impossible to resist. The siren used her song to lure men willingly to their deaths. Guillaume le clerc wrote from a moralist and Christian point of view and was eager to point out that men should not be deceived into sinful behaviour, 'becoming entangled in the snares of the evil one', because; "Then he attacks us, then he falls upon us, then he kills us, then he does us to death, just as syrens do to the mariners who sail the seas." Guillaume was happy to compare the mermaid with the Christian devil.

A little later in the same century, the encyclopedic bestiary of Bartholowmew Angelicus described mermaids as; "drawing shipmen to peril by the sweetness of song." In both Guillaume's and Bartholowmew's works it was considered that the mermaid lulled men into a trance-like sleep in order to seal their fate. Bartholowmew goes further and states that mermaids would be likely to rape the men she had captured before killing and devouring them. The song of the mermaid was, in fact, a powerful spell or enchantment, the ultimate lullaby!

In Homer's *Odyssey*, the hero Odysseus has to face the perilous voices of the sirens. To survive he takes heed of advice given by the goddess Circe and plugs the ears of his men with beeswax. Odysseus himself is tied to the mast of his ship so that he might hear the sirens' song without being lured into their clutches.

Today, the term 'siren' is linked with the mermaid. In medieval bestiaries she often goes under the caption 'syren' or 'siren'. In French folklore mermaids are 'Les sirenes', but it is worth mentioning here that the siren of Ancient Greece was, originally, an entirely different creature. Odysseus was faced with passing their rocky abode, and although Homer does not describe them, only their deadly voices, the creatures he encountered would have been part woman, part bird. How the sirens metamorphosed into mermaids will be discussed later.

It has already been mentioned that the mermaids of the Channel Islands would sing before storms. It was said that their song lured the sailors onto the rocks where they could prey on them, and in Sark and Guernsey at least, the song of the mermaid was actually thought to cause the storms. The fishermen of the Channel Islands clearly faced the same perils as Odysseus, and interestingly enough the mermaid is known locally as the siren.

The song of the mermaid is said to induce madness in the Faeroes; fishermen would follow Odysseus's example and plug their ears to prevent the sound reaching them. In Skye, madness came to those that heard the song of the Maighdeann na Tuinne (maid of the waves). No fisherman would sail close to Spay's Cave, one of her particular haunts, for fear of hearing it. The belief that a mermaid's song heralded an approaching storm at sea was common in Cornwall, the example at Lamorna Cove has already been mentioned. The same was true elsewhere; at St.Malo in France it was only unlucky to hear a mermaid sing at night, a sure sign of bad weather. If she only sang during daylight hours those at sea would be safe.

In 1635 the writer John Swan published his work *Speculum Mundi*. In the book he theorises on the ability of the mer-folk to raise storms. Swan states; "...those sudden tempests are very strange and how they arise with such violent speed exceeds the bounds of ordinary admiration." Swan goes on to propose that the mermaids and 'men-fish' have the power of "the verie devils" According to Swan's theory the mermaids would set up a thickening of the atmosphere with the cacophony of their voices, and their violent rushing to and fro under the water would build up the waves from below, until a full blown storm would break out.

On the other side of the Atlantic, the Mic Mac people of eastern Canada believe that the song of 'The Halfway People' or Sabawaelnu (water-dwellers) presaged a storm. The Halfway People were human above the waist with the tail of a fish below. In Louisiana the entire Pascagoula tribe were enchanted by a mermaid's song and lured into the river. They were never seen again. The story of the Pascagoula and the mermaid is told later.

Although it was more usual for the song of the mermaid to herald a storm, sometimes it was just enough to see her, dancing on the waves, before the onset of a tempest. In many cases the mermaid herself was blamed for raising the storm, as John Swan's writing indicates. Her ability to control the weather and the waves is well documented in folklore.

In Welsh folklore the mermaid that appeared to the fisherman Pergrin, and bid him take up his nets immediately, was warning of an impending storm. Pergrin pays heed to the warning, even though the sea is flat calm, and sails for home. He is saved, but eighteen others lose their lives. Also from Wales is the story of the mermaid Nefyn, who can calm a storm at sea by whispering to the waves. The story of Nefyn, daughter of the sea-king is told later.

From further north comes an interesting example of a mermaid raising a story by unusual means. A Scottish mermaid, furious at being captured by a fisherman, begins to tie his net in knots. After the first two knots, the sky grows dark. On tying the third, the mermaid raises a storm that threatens to engulf the man's boat. Knot-lore in the weaving of spells is an ancient tradition in European witchcraft and has intimate links with goddess worship. The basis behind this particular piece of mermaid folklore may be very old indeed.

The Ben-Varrey of Man would sometimes warn fishermen of bad weather, much like the mermaid in the story of Pergrin. Waiter Gill, in *A Manx Scrapbook* (1929), mentions a Ben-Varrey that rose suddenly to the surface amongst some fishing boats and cried a warning; "Shiaull er thalloo!" or "Sail to land!" Those who heeded her cry were saved. Traditionally, the appearance of the Norwegian Havfrue heralded an approaching storm. In France the mermaid had the power to raise storms and sometimes went by the name 'Naguerite mauvais temps'. A French mermaid once raised a storm so powerful that twenty ships were blown ashore.

As well as the power to raise storms, the mermaid was much feared for her ability to utter curses upon those who had wronged her or her kin.

At Padstow in Cornwall a mermaid is said to be responsible for the creation of a sand-bar, treacherous to shipping, called 'The Doombar'. The harbour at Padstow was once deep enough for ships to anchor, so the legend goes, but is now choked with sand. The mermaid's curse came about after she was shot at by a local man. A similar tale is told about the harbour at Seaton. On this occasion the mermaid is injured by a local sailor. Another version says that the man simply insulted her, obviously a risky thing to do! In Galloway, a mermaid who is insulted by a local woman lays a curse of barrenness upon her and her house. The story goes that the mermaid would sit upon a favourite granite rock just off-shore and sing as she sat combing her hair. A local woman, and devout Christian, was offended by the sight and sound of such an obviously pagan creature. The mermaid's flagrant and shameful exhibition was an insult to the good Christian folk thereabouts. The woman swore to herself that she would put a stop to the mermaid's behaviour and one day she has the granite 'mermaid's chair' toppled into the water. The incensed mermaid utters her curse and it results in the woman's line eventually dying out. This tale comes via R.H. Cromek's *Remains of Nithsdale & Galloway Song* (1810). A similar tale from Ayrshire is told later, but in *The Mermaid of Knockdolian*, the ending has a more sinister twist.

The curse of the mermaid always seemed to be particularly potent. Few tales tell of the victims managing to avoid their fate. However, one tale from the west coast of Ireland tells of a fisherman named Shea who kills a mermaid. With her dying breath the mermaid curses Shea and all his descendants. The curse took the form of an avenging wave, or bore, and Shea himself was drowned by it. Shea's descendants, however, learnt to read the waves and knew how to avoid the deadly bore. They had effectively escaped the mermaid's curse, something that few had ever managed.

If the mermaid has the power to utter deadly curses, she also has the power to grant wishes. Grateful mermaids would often repay acts of kindness with magical gifts or the bestowing of certain powers.

The well-known Cornish folk-tale, *Lutey and the Mermaid* has been mentioned already with reference to the power of the mermaids' comb. The mermaid encountered by Lutey has been stranded by the receding tide, and the act of kindness is the man returning her to the sea. The mermaid grants Lutey three wishes in return, and because he chooses unselfishly, he and his family thrive. However a warning in dealings with fairy-folk is evident here; in a twist to the tale, every nine years a descendant of Lutey's is lost at sea.

In Ireland a popular wish granted by the mer-folk was protection from storms at sea. This type of wish granted to sailors and fishermen harks back to a far more ancient, pre-Christian tradition of offerings and invocations made by seafarers to the sea-goddess and sea-god in order to obtain protection or their voyages.

The ability of the mer-folk to grant wishes was well known in Scotland and sailors would sometimes actively try to capture mermaids and force them into granting them in return for their release. But tricking or forcing a mermaid into anything is a risky business (as it is with any of the fairy-folk). Human greed is frowned upon and no good will come of wishes demanded in this way.

In Ireland and Scotland (including Shetland and Orkney) various families claim a mermaid amongst their ancestors. Often the belief was that special gifts bestowed by the mermaid would be passed down through the generations. The same is claimed by several Cornish families. Mysterious powers, such as protection from drowning, are inherited from mermaid ancestry.

One wish sometimes asked of the mermaid is the ability to foretell the future. One imagines that this was an easy thing for the mermaid to grant, as the power of prophesy is one of her own talents. In Norway, the prophetic power of the mermaid was well known, and fishermen believed that their offspring were particularly good at this. If caught, the mer-children, (or marmaeller as they were called locally), were taken home and quizzed on the future.

In 1755 The Bishop of Bergen, Erik Pontoppidan, wrote of his belief in the mermaid. In his work *Natural History of Norway* he describes how the Havmand and Havfrue were often seen in the North Sea and were undeniably real. Pontoppidan describes how fishermen would capture young mermaids and give them milk to drink, in the hope that this would encourage them to foretell something of the future. Whether they did so or not, the young mermaids were never kept for more than twenty-four hours by the superstitious fishermen, and were always released unharmed.

In Scotland, a mermaid that was seen washing blood-soaked clothing was foretelling the death of thirty six people. After this ominous portent the roof of the local church collapsed and the thirty six were killed. In this folk-tale a mermaid seems to be taking the place of the Bean-nighe, or 'washing woman', a variant of the Banshee. The Bean-nighe is known in both Scotland and Ireland, and is seen by desolate streams and pools washing the blood-stained garments of those about to die. In some cases the Bean-nighe is said to have webbed feet, indicating that she may be considered a water-spirit, and like the mermaid she will grant three wishes if one can get between her and the water. But to try this and fail is to court disaster. The Bean-nighe are said to be ghosts of women who have died in childbirth. They are destined to perform their task until the time when they would have died naturally. In the Middle Ages tradition amongst sailors spoke of a mermaid predicting the fate of a crew in the event of a storm. During a storm, if a mermaid was seen playing with a fish, she would be watched carefully. If the mermaid threw the fish away from the ship, all would be saved, but should she throw the fish on deck, some or all of the crew were sure to perish.

Two mermaids playing in the River Danube are forced to reveal what the future held for Hagen and his knights in the *Nibelungenlied*. Hagen and his men hide the garments of the mermaids, (or more accurately - *'wasser-nixen'* or water-spirits), and withhold the clothing until they agree to tell what the future has in store. Unfortunately for Hagen, the mermaids predict death for both him and his men should they cross the river.

A little-known talent of the mermaid is her knowledge of herb-lore, but various references are made to this skill in European folklore. In the Firth of Clyde a mermaid once appeared in the water as a funeral was passing by. A young, local girl had died of consumption and the mermaid lamented.

> *"If they wad drink nettles in March,*
> *and eat muggons in May,*
> *sae mony braw maidens*
> *wadna gang to the clay"*

'Muggons' is the mugwort or southernwood. The mugwort is *Artemisia vulgaris* and is sacred to the fish-tailed Artemis. It is also linked to the moon in herb-lore. On the coast of Galloway a mermaid advises a young man that he may cure his young lady, who is dying of consumption, if he makes up an extract of mugwort and gives it to her as a tonic. The man takes the advice and the young woman recovers.

Sir John Rhys relates the Welsh tale, *The Physicians of Mydfai* in his *Celtic Folklore* (1901), which tells of a water-fairy, (one of the Gwragedd Annwn) that passes her knowledge of herb-lore and medicine on to her three mortal sons. Her sons become famous physicians, known far and wide for their unusual skills. Like the magical gifts passed to humans by mermaids, the skills bestowed by the water-fairy are passed down through the generations of the family. The story of the physicians of Mydfai is told later, in the tale *The Lady of Llyn Y Fan Fach*.

Another, less well known, attribute of the mer-folk is their ability to sink ships simply by leaping on board and 'becoming heavy'. Mermen are especially good at this, and Pliny mentions this peculiar talent in his *Natural History*, (a monumental work of thirty-seven volumes and written in the first century AD). Pliny writes, on the 'mere-man';

"...that in the night season he would come out of the sea aboard their ship: but look upon what ever part soever he settled, he waid the same downe, and if he rested and continued there any long time he would sink it clean." Pliny also describes mermaids

as having rough skin, "*Skaled all over.*" A far cry from the beautiful white-skinned maiden of the waves.

Already mentioned is John Swan's work *Speculum Mundi* .... There too we find mention of the merman's curious ability to sink ships by climbing aboard at night and depressing one end by suddenly becoming heavy.

The merman, in general, shares the abilities of his mate; controlling the weather and the waves, avenging wrongs, but sometimes showing gentler traits such as granting wishes and even going as far as befriending humans, (as in the case of the merrow or the havmand). The Dooinney-Marrey (the Manx merman) has been known to warn fishermen of bad weather, and sometimes helps them find herring shoals. However, on the whole, the merman seems less interested in mankind than the mermaid, and correspondingly appears less in folklore. The mermen were often uglier than the mermaids, and were certainly wilder; "personifying the stormy sea" according to the great folklorist Katherine Briggs. Mermaids would often fall in love with humans, but not so the mermen, who never actively sought a human bride. However the merman could be amorous and sometimes, like the Greek triton, he would come ashore and force himself upon some luckless woman.

The Cornish merman has been accused of cannibalism, (eating his own children), although the Manx merman (the Dooiney-Marrey) is described as an affectionate father in *The Baby Mermaid*, a tale told by Dora Broome in her *Fairy-tales from the Isle of Man* (1951).

Apart from the devouring of men and cannibalism of their own kind, some mer-folk are said to have vampiric tendencies. Mermaids living in Lake Tanganyika and the Lukuga River in Burundi are greatly feared as vampires. Local people call them the *Mambu mutu*. The Mambu mutu drink the blood of their victims and then eat their brains.

For the most part, the folklore of the mermaid portrays her and her mate as the villains of the piece. Fewer tales exist where the mermaid shows her benevolent side or is even the victim. She is most certainly a pagan creature, descended from the oldest sea deities, but her folklore persisted and evolved with the Christian era, until the main theme of her folklore was her longing for final salvation, the desire for a soul and a place in the Christian heaven. This became the case in the folk-tales of other fairy types and with this 'Christianisation' the fairies began to slowly die out, or in more accurate terms, they simply started to fade away.

But the mermaid remained; her image endured and her relationship with the Christian church developed. This last matter is discussed in a later chapter, but next we will turn to the mermaid's kin. The next chapter is a small selection of sea, lake and river spirits from Europe and the rest of the world.

Chapter 2
Mer-folk and Other Water-Spirits

Sea-Trows

The word 'trow' is a corruption of the Scandinavian 'troll', and the trows of Shetland and Orkney are not unlike their Norse cousins. A type of trow that lives in the sea (and sometimes marshes), seems to be a cross between the mer-folk and the seal-people (or selkies).

Like the selkies, the sea-trows have a skin which they use to pass unhindered through the water and, like the selkies, without this skin they are helplessly trapped on land. The skin is described by Dr Samuel Hibbert in his *Description of the Shetland Isles* (1822), as that of a marine creature "*...capable of existing in the sea.*" One shape taken by the sea-trow is that of a beautiful woman or man above the waist, but with a fish's tail below. What distinguishes them from the local mermaids is that the sea-trows can remove their 'fishy parts' and come on land in human form. In the folk-tale '*Gioga and Ollavitinus*' the skins of the sea-trows are those of seals, but how one distinguishes a sea-trow in a seal skin from a selkie is anyone's guess.

Sea-trows love to bathe in the moonlight and cast their skins about them on the beach. It is at this time that they are most at risk, and their skins are sometimes stolen by men who then gain control over the trapped sea-trow.

Once Christianity had taken hold in Shetland the sea-trows had become fallen angels, not bad enough for hell, that had taken refuge beneath the sea. This tradition was shared by the selkies, and fairy folk in general. According to Dr Hibbert, the sea-trows lived *"far below the regions of fishes, and in pearly and coralline habitations."* But sometimes sea-trows frequented the marshes, where they waited in order to lead travellers astray.

Morgen

In Breton lore the morgen is a beautiful seductress who lives beneath the sea in a marvellous palace. By day the morgen slumbers beneath the waves, but at night she surfaces to untangle her long blond hair with a golden comb. Her singing voice is irresistible to any who hear it, and men are drawn into the waters toward her, and their inevitable doom. The mere touch of the morgen is death. But worse still, to a Christian especially, the touch of the morgen removes the mark of baptism and condemns the soul to an eternity of wandering the cold seas. The morgen shares many characteristics of the mermaid, and is almost certainly one herself.

In volume I of his *Celtic Folklore* (1901), John Rhys suggests that the Breton morgen is probably the same creature as the Welsh morgan, originally a lake mermaid herself, but later found in the sea. In both cases the morgen/morgan is probably descended from a much older water goddess and has links with Morgan le Fey of Arthurian legend.

An old Breton legend explains the origin of the morgen and is explained later. It concerns Dahut, the daughter of King Gradlon, ruler of the legendary of Ys. The term 'morgen' (and 'morgan' probably comes from the old Celtic '*morigenos*', meaning 'born of the sea'. In Gaelic this is found as '*muirgen*' Sometimes the morgen goes by the name '*morverch*' in Brittany, the term meaning 'sea-daughter'

Ceasg

A Scottish name for the mermaid, the *'maighdean na tuinne'* or 'maiden of the waves'. The ceasg, (pronounced keeask), is described as a beautiful woman from the waist up, but with the tail of a young salmon below. Like the mermaid, she will grant three wishes if she is forced, but is generally thought of as a dangerous spirit and is best avoided. Skye fishermen feared the ceasg greatly, and with good reason.

A (presumably) gigantic ceasg once swallowed a young man but was tricked into regurgitating him by the beautiful harp playing of his sweetheart. The young man then managed to kill the ceasg by destroying the egg in which she had hidden her separable soul. This tale is told in full by Donald Mackenzie in *Scottish Folk Lore and Folk Life* (1935). In his work Mackenzie suggests that the ceasg may have once been a sea-goddess to whom sacrifices were made.

Ben-Varrey

The Manx mermaid, whose mate is the Dooinney-Varrey (or Dooinney-Marrey). The Ben-Varrey is a typical mermaid, (if there is such a thing) feared for her luring of sailors to their death, but has a gentler nature than most. She sometimes warns sailors of bad weather. A delightful tale tells of a baby Ben-Varrey that steals the doll of a little girl playing on the beach. The mother of the young mermaid rebukes her and gives her a pearl necklace to give to the little girl in compensation.

The Dooinney-Marrey is a friendly creature on the whole, far less wild and dangerous than the typical merman. He has more in common with the Irish Merrow and the Norse Havmand. The Dooinney-Marrey is also alleged to be an excellent father to his children.

Ben-varrey

Merrow

One name for the Irish mer-folk, 'merrow' is an anglicised form of 'morvadh' according to Thomas Crofton Croker. The merrow is also known as the 'murdhuacha'. As already mentioned, merrows were generally friendly creatures, especially the male. The beautiful female could be a little unpredictable, and heralded a storm with her appearance. For all his kindness, the male merrow is a very ugly creature, even somewhat frightening in appearance. He has green skin and hair, and sharp green teeth. His arms are short and flipper-like, and his nose long and red. The male merrow is not averse to a drink, and also has the ability to come ashore as a small, hornless bull. Both male and female rely on their magic cap, the 'cohuleen druith' or a magic red feather to live and move underwater. An excellent folk-tale concerning the relationship between a man and a male merrow is *The Soul Cages* and is told later.

Havmand/Havfrue

The Norwegian mer-folk. The Havfrue appears as a typical mermaid, and has the same general characteristics. The Havmand is the merman, and is a friendly and handsome creature with green or black hair and beard. In folklore the Havmand is not necessarily fish-tailed, and as well as living in the sea, he sometimes lives at the foot of a cliff or even in hills nearby.

The Seal-Folk

The mythology surrounding the seal is closely related to that of the mermaid, and in British and Scandinavian folklore at least, the two sometimes interact.

At a distance, the seal may have deceived many a super-stitious sailor into believing he was looking at a mermaid. The sleek shape and 'fishy' tail, coupled with mammalian features and large beautiful eyes could have easily caused an over-active

Havmund

imagination to see something more. As well as this, seals have the habit of basking on rocks, as do mermaids, and the sometimes 'musical' voice of the seal all add to the illusion. In times when the mer-folk were generally accepted as real, cases of mistaken identity must certainly have accounted for many sightings.

But the seal-folk have their own mythology. The Ancient Greeks believed that some seals concealed a woman beneath the skin. These seal-women would drown unwary swimmers, but would then weep over the victim's lifeless body. Even today, in Greece, a person crying false tears is said to be "crying like a seal". In Ancient Greek mythology was the seal-king god, Phocus. Through his union with a sea-nymph, the nereid Psmathe the Golden, the Phocian people claim descent.

Psmathe herself transformed into a seal to avoid the unwanted attentions of Aeacus, son of Zeus. Some early Phocian coins have seal designs engraved an them. The seal known to the Phocians and other Ancient Greeks would have been the Mediterranean Monk Seal (*Monachus monachus*), a species sadly rare today, with probably less than 500 individuals left.

Further north we find seal-folk mythology in Scotland and the islands, Ireland, The Isle of Man, Scandinavia, Iceland and various other places. Indeed the mythology occurs wherever those sea-faring Norsemen, the Vikings, had influence. The Vikings travelled widely and with them came their legends. Wherever they settled, their legends took root and grew.

The Great Grey Seal (*Halichaerus grypus*), or silkie, was believed to be a human in seal form. W.T. Dennison in his *Orcadian Sketchbook* (1880) wrote: "*Every true Norseman looks upon the seal as a kind of second cousin in disgrace.*"

In one version the grey seals are fallen angels condemned to live in the sea (as are the sea-trows). Another story explains that the seal-folk are a race of humans banished to the sea for their sins and forced to take the form of a grey seal. A variation on this tale, told in Sweden, is that the grey seals are descended from Pharoah's soldiers, drowned in the Red Sea. The bark of the grey seal is the cry "Pharaohl!, Pharaoh!"

The seal-folk were allowed to take on human shape, and come on land, only on certain nights of the year. This was on three full moons a year in the Hebrides, but only at Candlemas in the Faeroes and midsummer in Iceland. When they did come on land, the seal-folk would shed their seal skins and leave them scattered about on the beach. Then they would dance from sunset until dawn.

The Norsemen called the grey seal (and the seal-folk), 'silkies'. This name travelled with the Vikings to Shetland and Orkney where it became 'selkie' Further south, in the Hebrides and other islands, the seal-folk were the 'roane', this was also the Gaelic term for a seal. In all cases it was only the grey seal that could transform into human shape, the smaller common seal (Phoca vitulina) was entirely of the animal kingdom.

The magic skins of the seal-folk allowed them to appear as normal seals in the water, and were essential to their marine existence in much the same way as the magic caps, belts and feathers were to the mermaids. Once in their skins the seal-folk could travel through the water as easily as any seal, but if deprived of them they would be trapped on land, completely unable to return to the sea.

This forms the basis for the most common type of folk-tale told about them in Northern Europe. He who could steal the skin of a selkie maiden, could compel her to become his wife. On land, and in their human form, the female seal-folk were beautiful beyond comparison, far more so than any human woman. It was not unusual for a man to desire one for his bride. Should the opportunity arise, and the man clever enough, he could snatch up one of the skins that lay unattended on the rocks as the seal-maidens danced. The unlucky seal-maiden would have no choice but to marry the man. In folk-tales from Scotland, Ireland, Iceland and Scandinavia tales of this type are found.

Slight variations occur, but the outcome is always the same. Once the man has the seal skin, the seal-maiden is prevented from returning to the sea. No matter how much she cries and begs for its return, the man refuses and forces her to marry him. The seal-maiden becomes a good and loyal wife, (up to a point. She does continue to search for her skin). She usually has several children by her new husband, but her longing for the sea is greater than her love for them. One day she finds her carefully hidden skin and she leaves forever, finally returning to her natural element. Often in tales like this, the seal-maiden is torn between returning to the sea and leaving her offspring (and on rare occasions, her husband), but she always does so. In one variation the ending is slightly different, in that the seal-maiden returns to visit her children. She appears to one, or more, of her offspring on the beach and bestows some kind of secret knowledge on them. This 'return' of a fairy- bride is seen elsewhere in folklore, an example being the 'Physicians of Mydfai' mentioned earlier and told later. In this example the fairy-bride is a Welsh water-fairy, one of the Gwragedd annwn, and the secret knowledge is that of medicine and healing beyond mortal skills.

Once the seal-wife leaves her husband, he is usually just left to pine. But in one story from the Isle of Skye, a fisherman steals the skins of several seal-maidens who are then compelled to marry him and his companions. Eventually the fisherman feels pangs of guilt and returns the skins of all the seal-maidens. His companions make after their escaping wives, but when they try to prevent them reaching the sea, the men are turned to stone. The folklore of the 'fairy-bride' almost always follows the same general pattern. The union between man and fairy is always tinged with tragedy and loss; the marriages are doomed to fail. Folk-tales of this sort are found all over the world and are well represented in the Celtic and Scandinavian countries. In Teutonic folklore, the swan-maiden plays a central role in this

Water nymph

type of tale, and like the seal-maiden, has a magic skin (a feather cloak in this case) that allows her transformation. It is the theft of this cloak that causes her to marry a mortal man. In *The Science of Fairy Tales* (1891), E.S. Hartland analyses the swan-maiden legend and treats the seal-maiden legend as a variant of the same tale.

Tales concerning seal-men are rarer, (as are tales of mermen in relation to those of mermaids) but they are apparently amorous creatures that often ventured ashore to court mortal women, unlike the seal-maidens that never actively sought a mortal lover. Considering the other-worldly beauty of their normal mates, this seems to be an unusual state of affairs. The offspring of humans and seal-folk are always recognisable by webbed fingers and toes at birth. The webs were always cut by the midwife, but grew into horny excrescences, marking the individual as a child of the seal-people.

As in mermaid folklore, some old families claim to be descended from the seal-folk. The Clan MacCodrum of the Hebrides claim a seal-maiden in their family tree, and no member of the clan would ever dream of killing a seal. In Scandinavian countries certain families claim to be descended from unions between a family member and a seal-maiden. Traditionally, such families were excellent fishermen. In Orkney "men wi the horn on their hands and feet" were said to be descendants of Brita. Brita was the daughter of an Orkney laird and bore the children of a seal-man or selkie. Brita's children were born with webbed fingers and toes, but over several generations the webs turned to horny outgrowths on the hands and feet. The 'children of Brita' are described by David Thomson in his *The People of the Sea* (1954). In Ireland the Lees were said to be safe from drowning due to the seal-folk blood in their veins.

The seal-folk were always regarded as the gentlest of sea-spirits, much more so than the mer-folk. But just as a mermaid will avenge a death or injury to her kind or herself, so the blood of a seal-maiden spilt on the water will most surely raise a storm. The tale of *The Wounded Seal-Father* is told later, and illustrates the reaction of the seal-folk to the persecution of seals by a fisherman.

A last note on the seal-folk is to mention their interaction with mermaids. An interesting, but sad story from Shetland tells of a mermaid who sacrificed herself for a selkie. This story explains why the seal-folk consider themselves guardians of the mer-folk; warning them whenever there is danger, and sometimes paying with their own lives. *The Mermaid's Sacrifice* is told later.

Other Water-Spirits

Muilearteach
A form of the Scottish Cailleach bheur that lives in the water, (The Cailleach is a type of hag, and probably descended from an ancient crone goddess). The muilearteach is sometimes a sea-spirit with a reptilian as well as human form. She comes ashore and appears as an old hag with one eye and a blue/black face, but most horrifying of all is her ability to swell in size. She is known for raising storms at sea and is generally feared.

Brounger
Also from Scotland, this time the east coast. The brounger is a portent of storms at sea, and was probably once a weather-god of some kind.

Marool
Jesse Saxby, in 'Shetland Traditional Lore' (1974) describes the marool as a sea-demon that has a fish-like form. The marool appears amongst phosphorescent sea foam and during storms.

Fuathan

'The Fuathan' is a generic term in Scotland for a collection of (usually) malicious water-spirits. The Fuathan are sometimes connected with the sea, but more usually with lochs and rivers. Katherine Briggs lists Shellycoat, The Peallaidh, and the Fideal amongst the Fuathan, as well as others. The Fideal was female and personified the entangling water weeds that trapped men in bogs. She haunted Loch na Fideil in Gairloch and specialised in drowning people. Shellycoat had a coat of shells that rattled as he moved and gave him his name. He is described by Sir Waiter Scott as a lowland water-bogle that frequents freshwater streams. Shellycoat likes to trick and mislead travellers, but is relatively harmless. The Peallaidh (pyaw-le) is a highland form of the shellycoat.

Loireag

Traditionally a water-fairy from the Hebrides, but better known for her association with spinning and weaving. She is generally thought of as friendly.

Gwragedd Annwn

Welsh water-fairies associated with lakes and belonging to the Plant Annwn family of fairies ruled over by Gwyn ap Nudd The Gwragedd Annwn, (pronounced: gwrageth anoon), are as benevolent as they are beautiful and sometimes married mortal men. Various lakes in Wales are haunted by them, including Llyn y Fan Fach in the Black Mountains, the setting for the tale *The Physicians of Mydfai*, by Rees of Tonn. The unions between Gwragedd Annwn and men always end in failure as they do with the seal-maidens, and indeed any fairy-bride.

River-Spirits

Many rivers in the British Isles have a particular spirit of fairy type associated with them. Undoubtedly these river-spirits are sometimes descended from old river goddesses, but some are simply derived from tales invented to frighten children and keep them from the water's edge.

The River Ribble has an evil spirit called Peg O'Nell, said to be the unquiet ghost of a maidservant from Waddow Hall. Peg O'Nell demands a drowning every seven years and will take a human if a cat or dog has not been offered. Undertones of sacrifice to the river-goddess are evident here. Peg Powler from the River Tees, and Jenny Greenteeth from the various stagnant pools in Lancashire are evil water-spirits who specialise in drowning children. Both should be classed as 'nursery-bogies' according to Katherine Briggs, invented by nervous parents to keep children away from dangerous waters, but William Henderson in his *Folk-lore of the Northern Counties* (1879), describes Peg Powler as a Lorelei type spirit with green hair. Henderson also describes the foam regularly seen floating on the higher part of the Tees as "Peg Powler's suds". Also in the north of England we find Nelly Long-Arms and Grindylow, both said to drown and devour unwary children.

In Scotland, almost every loch, river, stream and pool has its own guardiar spirit (as with other Celtic countries). The Cuachag is a dangerous river-spirit from Glen Cuaich in Inverness-shire, The Eiteag from Glen Etive. Both are classed as Fuathan.

In the south of England we find spirits in the rivers of Cornwall and Devon. The Tamar is the abode of the nymph Tamara, and the Rivers Tavy and Taw that of two giants, suitors of the nymph. The giants turned into rivers to be with Tamara, but unfortunately for the Taw he chose the wrong route and flows away from her, whereas Tavy merges with her near the sea. Dartmoor is the mother of many rivers, most haunted by a spirit of some kind. Ogres are connected to the Erme and the Yeo, the latter, named Cutty Dyer, loves to drown passers-by. The River Dart is the main river of the moor, and legend says that the Dart must have one victim a year. Local people still say that the "cry of the Dart" is the water-spirit calling for its victim.

The river-spirits of the British Isles alone are too numerous to mention here, and the same can be said for the rest of Europe and many other places around the world. Their sheer numbers bear witness to the importance placed on the life-giving and life-taking waters by any nature based religion.

Unðíne

A generic term used for a water-spirit or fairy, coming from the Latin '*unda*', meaning a wave. The undines traditionally represent the element of water, and are described as living in sacred fountains and wells, lakes and rivers.

Asraí

The Asrai are water-fairies from the Wales/England border counties and could certainly be described as typical undines. If captured they have a tendency to melt away into a pool of water, their natural element,

Sjora

Swedish water-spirits associated with lakes and the open sea. Like mermen, the males are often aggressive and will capsize boats and, like mermaids, the females will warn sailors and fishermen of approaching bad weather. The Sjora have a world comparative to that on land; under the water they live on farms and have pastures with sea-cattle.

Mara-Halðða

A Lapp sea-spirit. In the Finnish epic, *The Kalevala*, a young girl called Aino is drowned and turns into a salmon. Aino lived in a palace at the bottom of the sea where she tended her fish-tailed cattle.

Undine

Water-Horses

Water-horses are included here as many, especially those from Britain and Scandinavia, have a human form, and so may be counted as a distant relative of the mermaid. The best-known of the Scottish water-horses is the kelpie. The kelpie frequents rivers and lochs, but is more common in the former. A kelpie that haunted the River Conan in Sutherland demanded an annual victim, and many folk-tales about kelpies are of this type, sometimes known by the motif 'the Time is come, but not the Man'. Kelpies are generally dangerous water-spirits, sometimes devouring people they have lured into the water. In their most common form, that of a young horse, they would often appear, saddled and bridled, by the water's edge; too tempting for a passing traveller. Once on the kelpie's back, the unfortunate victim would be unable to dismount and the kelpie would plunge with him into the water, where he would be torn to pieces. It was said that if a bridle, over which the sign of the cross had been made, could be put on a kelpie, he would be under the control of the man that had managed it, but this was a risky business indeed. If a man can steal the kelpie's own bridle, he can use it to work magic. Another curious attribute of the kelpie is its ability to elongate its back, in order to get more than one rider to mount it. Also, to merely touch a kelpie is to be stuck fast.

The water-horse goes under a variety of names; The Manx water-horse is the Cabyll-Ushtey and is usually seen in the form of a bluish-grey horse. It is second only to the Each Uisge of the Scottish Highlands in its ferocity and is greatly feared. The Each Uisge is probably the most dangerous of all the water-horses (according to Katherine Briggs) and haunts the sea and lochs. Both Each Uisge and Cabyll-Ushtey can appear as a young or old man in order to trick humans. In water-horse form both catch and devour people and livestock. The Each Uisge shares the kelpie's abilities to elongate its back, and make itself 'sticky'. Similar to, (or perhaps the same as) the Each Uisge is the Aughisky. This creature comes ashore, mainly in November, and can be ridden safely if it is kept away from the sea. Should the Aughisky catch a glimpse of its home, then the rider would be dashed headlong into the water and devoured. Aughisky were also known for devouring cattle. Another water-horse from the Isle of Man, and similar to the Cabyll-Ushtey, is the Glastyn. In his *A Second Manx Scrapbook* (1932), Waiter Gill describes the Glastyn in his human form as; a dark, splendid young man with flashing eyes and curling hair, but to be distinguished by his ears, which, though fine and delicate, are pointed like a horse's. Like the Scottish Water-horses, the Glastyn may be spotted for what he really is by dripping wet clothes.

In Shetland, the water-horse goes under a variety of names. He is the Noggle or Nuggle and appears as a small grey horse. The Noggle is far less dangerous than some of the others of his kind, and is satisfied in giving his victims a thorough ducking. Sometimes the Noggle is called the Shoopiltie, and another form, also found in Orkney, is the Tangle. The Tangle is far easier to spot than most other water-horses, as his coat is rough hair and seaweed, not at all sleek. The Tangle appears as an old man when in human form.

The Welsh water-horse is the Ceffyl-dwr. This spirit haunts rivers and has the peculiar ability to illuminate the area around itself with its own luminosity. Like its Scottish, Irish and Manx cousins its most common form is a small horse or pony, but a human form is not unknown. For a more detailed study of the water-horses the reader can refer to the excellent book 'Lake Monster Traditions' by Michel Meurger and Claude Gagnon.

Nack/Nokk

A generally dangerous water-spirit of rivers, lakes and waterfalls from the Scandinavian countries. 'Nack' is the Swedish name for this spirit, but in Norway he is called the 'Nokk', and in Iceland, the 'Nykur'. Where the Nack inhabits waterfalls, he is sometimes known as the 'fossegrim' (waterfall goblin). Nacks in rivers are sometimes called the 'stromkarl' (river men) Like British water-spirits, the Nack is often blamed for drownings, and served to warn children from dangerous waters. In Norway the Nokk sometimes lives in fjords and claims an annual victim.

The Nack and the Nokk usually appeared in human form, but sometimes came on land in the guise of a grey horse. In this sense they could be related to the Scottish kelpie or the Manx Cabyll-Ushtey. The Icelandic Nykur appears more often in his water-horse form, and can be spotted by his back-to-front hooves. Both Nack and Nokk are described as fine musicians, excelling at the fiddle and the harp. They will teach humans to play, but in return for passing on their skill they demand payment. The Nack asks only for meat, a black cat or some drops of human blood. If he does not get his requested item, he drown his pupil. Also, the music of the Nack is fraught with danger, and likened to that of the devil himself. The tale 'The Dancers who could not stop' illustrates this danger, and is told later.

In common with mermaid folklore that began to appear in the early Christian era, there are tales of the Nacks' longing for salvation and God's mercy. In the case of the Nack this is usually granted.

Nixe/Nix

The Nix of Germany is a water-spirit (wasser-nixen) of lakes and rivers and is more or less the same creature as the Scandinavian Nack. Both males and females appear in Teutonic folklore, the Nix being masculine, the Nixe feminine. The Nixe likes to sit on rocks combing her long hair, much like a mermaid. Rarely the Nixe is depicted as fish-tailed, but more often she is simply a beautiful woman, although she does share some characteristics with the mermaid, such as her mesmerizing singing voice and prophetic powers. Like the mermaid also, she has her malevolent side, and will drown young men

Nixe

she has lured into the water with her singing. In some rivers the Nix/Nixe demands a yearly sacrifice, and is often seen dancing on the surface of the water just before some unfortunate soul drowns. The Nixe is also said to imprison the souls of those she drowns (a habit of the Irish Merman or Merrow).

On land the Nixe can be spotted by her otherworldly beauty, but a more certain method is to examine her clothing; the hem of her skirt is always wringing wet. The Nix is even easier to spot, as his teeth are green. As with the mermaid and the Swedish Nack, the Nixe/Nix often desires salvation and a place in the Christian heaven, but unlike their Scandinavian counterparts, they are usually denied.

Lorelei

The Lorelei borrows her mythology partly from the mermaid, and partly from the siren of Ancient Greece. She is the water-nymph of the River Rhine, where she sits amongst the rocks and lures men to their doom (the word 'Lorelei' comes from the old German 'Lur' meaning 'to lurk' and 'Lai' meaning 'rock'). It is the beautiful, but deadly singing voice of the Lorelei that is irresistible to those who hear it, and like her cousin, the mermaid, she likes to sit and comb her long hair as she sings.

Dracs

The Dracs of France haunt rivers, beneath which they live in submerged caverns. In their human form the Dracs are beautiful maidens who could come on land. At other times the Dracs would take the form of gold rings and float down the river. Any woman or child (their favourite prey) attempting to grab the rings would be seized and drowned. Alternatively the victim would be taken beneath the water to serve the Dracs in their caves. Often, human women would be taken to care for Drac children, or to act as midwives.

The Dracs who lived in the River Rhone once took a woman to look after their children. The woman stayed with the Dracs in their caverns for some weeks, but one day got the opportunity to return to the surface, and made her way home. Her husband greeted her, but was astonished at her story, telling her she has been away for years. Tales of fairy abduction are common in folklore and a central element to the tales is always the time difference between the human world and the fairy realm.

Throughout Europe many other water-spirits occur in sea, lake, rivers, streams and marshes. Wells, springs and pools are frequently haunted, and it seems that the size of a stretch of water is no obstacle to the elementals. Many water-spirits, like the river spirits of Britain, are specific to a particular location, and are too numerous to list. Of course the same is true for the rest of the world, wherever there is water, there are water-nymphs, fairies or even fish-tailed women. A few examples are listed below.

Russia

Mermaids were known to Ukraine mariners and were said to appear in rough seas, when they would sing before the storm. In Estonia a folk-tale of the 'Melusine' type tells of a farmer who marries a mermaid, but tragedy followed after the breaking of a taboo, ('Melusine' is told later). The mermaid told the farmer that a condition of their wedlock was that he should give her complete privacy on Thursdays. For a time the farmer respected his wife's wishes, but eventually curiosity got the better of him and he spied on her. The horrified farmer saw his new wife in her mermaid form, and having broken her 'fairy taboo', she left him and returned to the sea. In a twist to the Estonian tale, once the mermaid dives into the sea, the farmer ages on the spot and dies.

Rusalka

The Rusalka are Russian water-nymphs, but they are also found elsewhere in Eastern Europe. Rusalkas are female (considered under Christianity to be unbaptized girls who have died) and are described as beautiful maidens with long green hair. They haunt the rivers, where they will drown those they can lure into the water, and if the victim is a man, they will sometimes ravish him before he is dragged under. Rusalkas are said to be able to control the weather, and will come on land from time to time to dance in grain fields. When they do this the grain increases in vigour and grows well. In Slavonic custom 'Rusalka Week' is a week in the year when it is very unwise to swim in any river.

Vodyany

Male water-spirits in Russian and Eastern European folklore, they are said te rule the Rusalka. The Vodyany is related to the German Nix and the Swedish Nack. In appearance they are said to be ugly and fearsome, but they have been known to marry human women, who must then live with their otherworldly husbands in their underwater homes. Like the merman the Vodyany can control storms and will destroy fishermen and sailors. They will then collect the souls of those they have killed and keep them in jars. But with typical fairy perversity, they will sometimes aid people and are considered to bring good luck in these circumstances. Like the Nix, the Vodyany can be spotted on land by their dripping wet clothing; they leave damp patches wherever they have been sitting. They are also considered to be shape-shifters, and can take the form of a fish, or even a naked woman with long, wet hair.

Vodní-Panny

Water-nymphs with beautiful singing voices with which they lure men to their doom. The vodni-panny live in marvellous crystalline palaces beneath the water, and are described by Jan Machal in 'Myths of All Races: Slavic' (1918) as being tall, sad and pale.

Also from this part of the world are the many water-spirits of Finno-Ugric mythology. Examples are the Va-Kul who are malevolent and can be male or female and the Vu-Kutis who are water-spirits who are said to cure diseases.

Inòía

The Vedic scriptures describe the god Matsya, the first avatar (or incarnation) of Vishnu, as a god in fish-form. He is often depicted as simply fish-tailed; the first merman of India. Indian folklore is rich in tales of water-spirits, such as the Apsara who could be considered minor deities.

Apsara
The Indian water-nymphs or undines, originally produced by the 'churning of the ocean' (the Vedic deluge myth). The ancient Sanskrit Vedas mention the Apsaras' earliest home were the rivers, pools and fords. These nymphs are traditionally described as beautiful women, and bear some resemblance to the Greek nereids (who can also be considered minor deities). Like mermaids Apsaras were credited with prophetic powers, and one in particular was named Caksusi, the name meaning 'clairvoyant'. The Apsaras are often depicted dancing, and are known for their great love of music.

Jalparí
The Punjabi water-fairies. In common with the more malevolent Indian mer-folk the Jalpari would lure men into the water, or lie in wait for them. Once captured, if the man rejects the Jalpari's advances, she will drown him. If the man allows himself to be seduced, he may escape with his life.

Naga/Nagína
Described by some as lake mermen and mermaids respectively, although they are usually represented with serpent and not fish-tails, ('nagina' meant snake-maiden). Although they

represent the element of water, the Naga and Naginas sometimes live in subterranean caverns. They also occur in lakes, pools and sometimes the sea, living in underwater palaces. Both can be both destructive and helpful as far as humans are concerned. The Naga are also found in Malaya, Java, Thailand and Cambodia.

Africa

Africa has a strong tradition of water-spirits, and almost every pool, stream, river and lake has a resident spirit living in it. The lakes and rivers especially, are thought by many tribes to be the dwelling places of the dead. The mermaid is well known in Africa; The Kpelle people of Liberia have a tradition of the 'Water People '. These spirits have human torsos and heade (usually with long hair), but the tails of fish from the waist down. In Jan Knappert's *African Mythology* (1990), the Kpelle water-people are described as often sunning themselves on rocks, and the belief is that they will make a man rich if he has the courage to ask them for money.

In the Congo, Lake Matamba is said to be inhabited by dark-skinned mermaids with long hair and large fingernails. The Lake Matamba mermaids are said to be mute and fairly harmless. The far more sinister Mambu Mutu, the vampiric mermaids of Lake Tanganyika, have already been mentioned and lake mermaids are also found in Zambia and Nigeria.

The Njuzu of Zimbabwe are described as 'human-headed fish' The Karanga people believe the Njuzu to haunt all lakes, pools and marshes and that they are the guardians of pure water (an especially important element in Africa). In some cases the Njuzu will appear as beautiful maidens in order to lure young men into the water, where they drown them. In more recent times polluted waters and industrial noise have caused the Njuzu to leave their traditional homes. When they do so, they take the form of terrible, destructive tornadoes and leave devastation in their wake. In times past children sacrificed to the water-gods were thought to become Njuzu.

The Bisimbi are the water-nymphs of the Congo. They are found in wells, pools and at the sources of rivers. Sometimes they are described as being made of water and are often seen as mist hovering over the surface. The Bisimbi are dangerous and will drown swimmers. Strangely they are also thought to be responsible for skin diseases.

In the folklore of the Nubians of Sudan we find the Dogir; water-spirits that live in the River Nile. The Dogir capture human women to make them their wives, but in some areas the Dogir are said to eat their captives. Swahilj water-spirits called the Afriti are dangerous to swimmers, who they drag under and drown.

China & Japan

The mermaid is known in China, and like their European counterparts they are skilled healers with an extensive knowledge of herb-lore. A Chinese folktale is told about a mermaid who had hung her clothes on a tree while she bathed in a well. A farmer crept up on the mermaid and stole the clothes, thus forcing her to remain with him and become his wife. The tale goes on to tell how the mermaid bears the farmer two children, but finally leaves him by escaping on a cloud. The central theme of the stolen clothing giving power over the mermaid is a variation on the type of mermaid/seal-folk tale told in Northern Europe.

Water-spirits are numerous in China; In common with many other cultures around the world, each river has its own spirit or deity. The Apsara are found here as well as in India, and the five Dragon-kings and their wives rule the seas. The Dragon-Kings and Queens are also part of Japanese mythology, and the mermaid is common. The 'hairy' mermaid, the Mujima and the shark-tailed merman, the Samebito have already been mentioned. Another type of Japanese mermaid is the Ningyo, which haunt the waters around Taiyan Island. The Suijin are water-nymphs not unlike the Greek nereids, and the Senjo are sea-fairies that live within a fabulous undersea mountain.

The Pacific

Not surprisingly the world's largest ocean has a rich mythology concerning sea-gods, goddesses, mermaids, sea-nymphs and fairies. Many seafaring adventures occur in Pacific mythologies and the mermaid is well known through-out the innumerable islands. In many of the island mythologies the earliest gods and goddesses were fish and the first people were mer-folk.

The mermaid of the Philippines has long golden hair. Local folklore says that if you can pluck three hairs from a sleeping mermaid (which luckily she seems to spend a lot of her time doing), then she will be in your power and will ensure that your plans prosper. All this must be done in complete secrecy or the spell will be broken.

In the creation mythology of Polynesia the fish-god Ika-Tere created all living things, including mermaids and mermen (although in this case the fish/human split was down the middle. The left-hand side of the Polynesia mermaid was human and the right-hand side was a fish). From these mer-folk all humans were descended.

In an almost identical legend, the ocean-god Tangaro (often depicted as a giant fish), gave birth to mermaids and mermen. These mer-folk eventually lost their 'fishy' nature and became totally human in order to populate the land. In the creation mythology of the Cook islands the creatress goddess Varima Te-Takere, (The woman of the Very Beginning) shapes the first man, Vatea, who is a type of merman. Vatea also has this human/fish split down the middle. In Eastern Java, the ocean-goddess was known to employ many mermaids and mermen as servants in her palace at the bottom of the sea.

In Maori myth, Ngarara is a sea-goddess, and may be a mermaid goddess as she is described as a beautiful woman from the waist up, but with a tail below. Ngarara sometimes comes on land, and may have actually been a sea-serpent goddess in the same way as the Babylonian Tiamat. Ngarara tends to be thought of as a sea-demoness.

Other types of water-spirit abound in the Pacific region. In the Gulf of Thailand, the Sam Muk sends storms to wreck fishing boats if sacrifices to him are neglected. The Sam Muk is said to be the shade of a young girl who killed herself for love. The spirit of the girl haunts a deep cave on an island named after her (or vice versa?). In the cave, the Sam Muk guards a huge treasure hoard.

The Ponaturi are the Maori sea-fairies, but they are also described as 'the ogres of the ocean' and are often at war with the heroes of Maori mythology. The Ponaturi come ashore only at night as they are killed by sunlight. Also from New Zealand are the Toniwha, benign water-spirits who live in rivers, ponds and wells. In the latter their job is to ensure that the water stays fresh. A similar job is undertaken by the river-spirits of Malaysia. Rice is scattered on the water by Malay fishermen, as offerings in exchange for their protection. The Hantu-Ayer are Malaysian water-spirits from the South China Sea. The Hantu-Ayer sometimes appear as fire over the water, and fishermen tie palm twigs on the top of their masts to stop these spirits from perching on them.

Many Pacific islands have legends of dangerous sea-spirits, and these are considered demons in some places, (such as the Pua Tu Tahi of the Tahitians). Web-footed, water-dwelling humans are found in New Britain, and in the Soloman Islands the Adaro is a malevolent merman-type spirit. The Adaro have tail-fins on their feet, gills behind the ears, a shark's fin and the pike of a swordfish on their heads. The Adaro are generally feared as they will attack fishermen.

The New World

The mermaid and merman were most certainly familiar to many of the indigenous peoples of both North America and Canada. She is mentioned in the folklore of the Iroquois, Ottawa and Mic Mac nations of Canada. The Apache knew her, as did the Shawano east of the Mississippi, the Lillooet of British Columbia and the Cree of Oklahoma.

The Shawano, in particular, have a legend of a merman deity that led their people across the sea to America, more of this is told in the next chapter. In Lillooet tradition, a local river was inhabited by the 'water-mysteries', who appeared in the form of fish-tailed men. In an Amerindian folk-tale from Cape Cod, a sea-giantess is described as having long hair, a snow white body and a sea-green tail. This description is not unlike those found in Celtic mythology of giant mermaids. Further north, the Inuit feared the merman, called Inue, for his ability to raise storms. Malevolent water spirits called the Atalit collect the souls and bodies of the drowned, in a similar fashion to the merrows of Ireland and some other mer-folk. The Penobscot believe in the Wanagemeswak, virtually invisible water-spirits, and the Gahongas of the Iroquois are dwarf-like beings that dwell in the water and the rocks. The Ojibiwa of Lake Superior called these dwarf mer-folk Maymaygwayshi. They have children's bodies, are two or three feet high, and have hairy faces. The Maymaygwayshi live behind or inside waterside rocks.

There is a merman-type creature known from Brazil called the Igpupiara (water-dweller), This is a particularly dangerous water-spirit by all accounts, which kills men by constricting them in a vice-like grip. The Igpupiara then eats the eyes, nose, genitals and the tips of the fingers and toes. The Igpupiara wails and moans in a mournful way whenever it kills, in a similar way to the Greek seal-women that cry and wail after they have drowned a swimmer.

In the New World, as in the old, water-spirits are found wherever there is water. The water-spirit folklore of the indigenous peoples of Canada, North America and South America is rich and varied. Only a very small sample is mentioned here.

Chapter 3
The Origins of the Mermaid

The home of the mermaid is traditionally seen as the sea, but it seems that she can show up wherever there is a body of water, salt or fresh, deep enough, mysterious enough or dangerous enough to have inspired a legend or folktale.

The mermaid is descended from the oldest sea-goddesses, who in turn personify the primeval ocean itself. The sea with its dark, mysterious depths, is seen as a powerful, archetypal symbol of the feminine. Psychoanalysis traditionally associates the sea with the archaic concept of woman as mother and lover; the sea is the mother of all life. Science itself tells us that all life sprang from the sea. In some form or another all the great Pagan religions connect water with fertility, and hence its feminine nature. The seas of the world are the womb of the first great mother-goddess. But the sea also represents 'the abyss' that can drag us down and drown us in its unfathomable depths.

The mermaid can exhibit both the life-giving and sexual nature of the waters, but at the same time can, like the abyss, be dangerous and deadly.

In his book *The Coming of the Cosmic Christ* (1988) Matthew Fox equates the ocean with the womb of the great goddess. Fox points out that Wisdom is represented as a "feminine, maternal figure, the Great Mother who emerges fron the sea". The mythologies of some cultures tell of a mighty sea-deity that arises from the water to pass wisdom to the people. Fox goes on to suggest that the archetypal sea-goddess represents a reawakening of human spirituality, in other words, a re-emergence of the feminine sub-conscious in Jungian terms, and the wisdom of enlightenment.

In Assyro-Babylonia, Tiamat, the great sea-serpent goddess, personified the chaotic primeval ocean, from whence came all life, and to where all living things returned in death. The Ancient Egyptian goddess Neith was regarded as the first waters of chaos and mother of the gods. In Ancient Greece, Tethys, the sea-goddess and daughter of Uranus and Gaia. was said by Homer to have created the gods and all living beings. In Persia, the Ahurani ('waters') were life-producing water-goddesses.

But what of the masculine? The mermaid, after all, has a mate. Sometimes the sea-goddess is fertilized by a sky-god. In the Finnish epic, *The Kalevala*, it is Ilmater, the 'Mother of the Waters', that creates the heavens, the earth the sun and the moon. She is impregnated by the divine east wind, and gives birth to the first man. Variations on this theme of creation are found all over the world. Rising patriarchies created the sea-gods, but the underlying feminine nature of the watery realms is inextricable, and it is from these primeval waters that we can trace the origins of the mermaid.

To the Gaelic Celts the sea was connected with a sense of primeval ancientness, and although Celtic tradition has left no native record of creation myth, they would most certainly have had one. The names of many Celtic deities are not recorded, due to their predominantly oral tradition but sea-goddesses and gods would definitely have been important. The wealth of mermaid and water-spirit folklore from Celtic countries, certainly suggests this.

Of the major Celtic deities, Domnu, a goddess of the Fomor, was possibly a sea-goddess, at least in origin. Domnu appears to have signified 'the abyss' of the deep sea. The Fomor them-selves were said to live under the sea. They were the offspring of 'chaos and old night', and the sea-demons of Irish mythology. The Fomor dwelt in the mysterious undersea realm of Lochlann, where they were ruled by their king, the ancient and shadowy sea-god, Tethra.

The traditional enemies of the Fomor were the Tuatha de Danaan; the people of the goddess Danu. The Tuatha were considered to be gods themselves, and amongst their number was Manannan mac Lir, a sea-god. Manannan was known in the Isle of Man (from where the island takes its name), and Ireland, but was called Manawyddan, son of Llyr, in Wales. Manannan is not depicted as fish-tailed, and so cannot be considered a model for the Celtic merman. He would ride the waves in his magical, self-propelled ship; 'Wavesweeper', and is also asociated with the Celtic otherworld.

Another Celtic sea-god is the Welsh Dylan, who "...*made for the sea, immediately upon his birth, and swam like a fish, taking on the very nature of the sea itself*". It was said that he swam so well that no wave broke under him, (from the *Mabinogion*). Another sea-god, who may have been the same as Dylan, is Enoil. His name persists in Cornwall as St. Endellion.

For Celtic sea-goddesses we have to look a little harder. Certainly, water-spirits associated with rivers and lakes are remembered in legend. The river goddess Tamesis gives her name to the River Thames, Tamara the River Tamar. The Dee is translated in old Celtic as 'the goddess'. The Boyne of Ireland is named after the goddess Boann. Wells and springs have their own associated spirits in many cases, and in Celtic lore, women are traditionally the guardians of such places; they were the true dwellings of the water-goddess. Two well-known legends illustrating this deserve a mention here. The first is the story of the Irish mermaid Liban, daughter of Eochaic of the Fir Bolg and Etain of the Tuatha de Danaan. *The Tale of Liban* is mentioned (in a Christianized form), in the 17th century work, *Annals of the Kingdom of Ireland* compiled by the Four Masters.

In the year 90 AD a sacred well, traditionally guarded by a woman, was neglected and overflowed with catastrophic results. The ensuing flood formed a great lake, called firstly 'The Lake of the Copse', but now known as Lough Neagh. In the flood, Eochaid and all his family were overwhelmed and drowned, except his two sons Curman and Conang and his daughter Liban. Liban and her pet dog were swept away by the flood waters and into an underwater cave. She stayed in the cave, with just her little dog for company, for a year, but then grew weary of her prison beneath the waters, and prayed to God to turn her into a salmon, so that she might leave.

God took pity on the girl and gave her the tail of a salmon, but he left her in human form from the waist up. Her little dog, he transformed into an otter. Liban swam the seas as a mermaid for three hundred years. During this time the missionary saints converted Ireland to Christianity, and so it was that Beoc, a clergyman of St. Comgall, was sailing to Rome from Ireland when he heard sweet singing from beneath the waves. Beoc thought that he must be hearing the voice of an angel, but Libar spoke to him and revealed herself. Liban asked Beoc to arrange a meeting for her with St.Comgall and he did so. Liban was drawn from the sea in the nets of the Saint's boat and taken to land, where the clergymen of St.Comgall half filled the boat with water to enable her to survive.

Liban was given the choice of immediate death, so that she might enter heaven, or to live on land for three hundred years and enter heaven after this. Libar chose to die straight away and St.Comgall baptized her in the name Muirgen ('born of the sea'). Liban then entered heaven and was counted from then on as one of the holy virgins.

Jean Markale, in *Women of the Celts* (1975), suggests that it is Liban herself who is supposed to guard the magic well, and through her neglect it floods and kills most of her family. Ironically Liban herself escapes death in the flood. Markale suggests that the story represents the struggle between

Christianity and Paganism going on in Ireland at the end of the 5th century. Interestingly, in local belief, it was held that mermaids lived in Lough Neagh and this belief was still strong in the 19th century. Local people would shun the Lough at night, in fear of being taken by the 'mere-maidens'.

The second story comes from Brittany and is the legend of Ker-Ys and the mermaid Dahud-Ahes or Dahud. The story is another variation on the sacred well or fountain theme and the flooding of a town. Again, the elements of Paganisn are in conflict with Christianity.

Long ago there was a fine city on the coast, called Ys. Ys was ruled by King Gradlon of Cornwall. Ys was protected from the ravages of the sea by strong floodgates, to which only Gradlon had the key. Ys prospered, and the inhabitants grew wealthy. In time, all the poor were driven from the city, and rich citizens lived lives of luxury and debauchery, led on by the king's own daughter, Dahud. Dahud was a shameless and wanton woman, given over to the rites of paganism. King Gradlon, who was a good Christian man, often came into conflict with his daughter because of her behaviour, and one day she stole his floodgate keys. Dahud opened the gates, and Ys was engulfed by the sea. Kine Gradlon fled on his horse and escaped the flood, but Dahud threw herself at him and jumped on his horse. St.Gwenole, founder of the abbey of Landevennes, struck Dahud with his cross, and she fell off and disappeared beneath the surface of the water.

But Dahud did not drown, from that moment on she became a mermaid and can still be seen swimming with shoals of huge fish. Fishermen say that on very calm days, the city itself can be glimpsed beneath the waves Local legend says that "When the day of resurrection comes for Ker-Ys, the first man to catch sight of the church spire or hear the sound of the bell will become king of the city and all its domains" (A. Le Brat, *Legende de 1a mort en Basse-Bretagne*).

According to Markale, Dahud-Ahes comes from the ancient Breton *dagosatis* which means 'good witch'. Dahud-Ahes was probably an ancient Breton sea-goddess originally, and in the story she represents feminine rebellion against male (patriarchal) authority.

In the case of Liban, she is put in charge of a sacred well by her father King Eochaid, and disobeys him by neglecting her duties, causing the flood. Although in the tale of Dahud there is no well or fountain, it is the sea itself that is held at bay by a dedicated guardian (the King). When the guardianship changes, (in effect by Dahud taking the floodgate keys from her father), it is her irresponsible actions that cause the deluge. The underlying theme of both stories is in fact one and the same; it is the rebellion of the pagan sea-goddess against a patriarchal Christian authority.

Well and spring worship was widespread amongst the ancient Celts, and offerings were made at sacred springs for the cure of diseases and for the purpose of divination. Both these skills are sometimes attributed to the mermaid herself in European folklore, and tales of her actually residing in wells and springs are not unknown. Pagan traditions associated with wells still survive today; People still leave offerings of cloth (tied to a tree) at Madron Well in West Cornwall, in the hope that the well spirit will rid them of some affliction. Few people probably realise that by tossing coins into a wishing well they are continuing a pre-Christian, Iron-age tradition.

There are other survivals of Celtic water-spirit worship. At Samhain, Hebridians would pour libations of ale to the old sea-god Shoney. This they did to implore Shoney to send seaweed to the shore. The practice was also prevalent in Ireland, and continued in both places until well into the 19th century. In a similar way, fishermen would leave offerings of fish for the sea-bucca at Newlyn in Cornwall, to ensure future catches, In the same county, a model boat called the 'cock-dayka' was offered to the sea-spirit at St, Ives. In County Mayo, Northern Ireland fishermen would make a token sacrifice to the sea-goddess, with a 'Babog mhara' or 'sea-doll'

Amongst the gods and goddesses of Northern Europe are the sea-deities Aegir and his wife Ran. Although mermaid lore is strong in the Scandinaviar countries, Aegir and Ran were not fish-tailed, just as Manawyddan of Wales and Manannan mac Lir of Ireland were not. Aegir, in particular, is not dissimilar to the Ancient Greek Poseidon (who only acquired a fish's tail rather late in his 'career'). To the Norseman, Aegir personified the wild ocean, and the "jaws of Aegir" were responsible for devouring many ships. The sea-goddess Ran stirred up the waves and carried a gigantic net, in which she would capture the drowning men.

Aegir and Ran lived in a marvellous underwater hall with their nine daughters. The daughters of Ran and Aegir represented the waves, and were irresistible undines who would lure sailors to their doom. The daughters had names like Gjolp (howler) and Greip (Grasper). For all their fear of Aegir and Ran, the Norse sailors knew that, for those drowned at sea there would always be a warm welcome waiting for them in Ran's hall.

In Icelandic legend, if a drowned man appears at his own funeral feast, it is a sure sign that he has been welcomed by the sea-goddess herself. Sailors would be careful to always carry a piece of gold on their voyages, so that if the worst happened, they would not be entering Ran's hall empty-handed.

An Irish legend tells of nine sea-giantesses that personified the waves, in the same way as the daughters of Aegir and Ran. *The Tale of Ruad*, son of Rigdonn tells how Ruad was crossing the sea to Norway when his three ships came to an abrupt and dead stop. Ruad dived under the water to find out what had caused the problem, and found three sea-giantesses holding each ship. The giantesses seized Ruad and forced him into spending a night with each of them. After this he was allowed to go on his way and the ships were released. But before he left, the giantesses told Ruad that one of them would bear his child and that he must visit them on his return journey.

Ruad stayed in Norway for seven years, and then began his return journey to Ireland. He passed the place where the sea-giantesses lived, but kept going. The sea-giantesses discovered Ruad's treachery and set off after him, but try as they might, could not catch up with him. As Ruad's ships disappeared over the horizon, the furious sea-giantesses ripped off the head of the unfortunate child and hurled it after him.

Despite the huge amount of mermaid lore from Britain and Scandinavia, the search for the origins of the mermaid must, inevitably, take us much further back in time. The Celtic and Norse sea-deities, as mentioned above, were not fish-tailed, and for the first true mermaid goddess and merman god we must turn our attention to ancient Chaldea and Babylon.

The deities of the Sumerians, Phoenicians and the Assyro-Babylonians are complex and overlapping. Many of the Semitic gods and goddesses developed and became incorporated into the Greek, and hence Roman pantheons.

In ancient Chaldea we find the first merman god in recorded history; Ea the god of water, wisdom and magic. Ea was the son of the primeval creator goddess of the dark waters, Bau, and he may be as ancient as she. Ea was probably worshipped in his mermaid form as early as 5000 BCE by the Accadians, from whom the Babylonians originally derived their culture. Ea overlaps with other gods, such as Enki. Enki is a water god, cursed by the Earth Goddess Ninhursag, (emphasising the dangers of uncontrolled water), but the curse is lifted upon the intervention of other gods, (emphasising the benefits of controlled water).

The Syrians and Greeks knew Ea as Oannes, (a sculpture dating from the 8th century BCE shows Oannes as a merman, and was discovered in the palace of Sargon II, an Assyrian king). As Ea, he was the husband of the Earth-goddess Damkina, or sometimes the Chaldean sea-goddess Gasmu ('the wise'). Whether Gasmu was fish-tailed or not is unclear. Ea (Oannes) brought civilisation and wisdom to the people of Assyro-Babylonia, and he also taught them magic, (maybe a distant memory of the arrival of an advanced, sea-going race of people). As Oannes, he was said to be the husband of Atergatis (Derceto), a mermaid goddess. Amongst the children of Ea was Inanna, the goddess of springs, and the god Marduk who helped his father in the battle with the sea-serpent goddess, Tiamat.

Tiamat has already been mentioned as representing the primeval waters of chaos. In Assyro-Babylonian mythology she symbolised the salt waters of the Earth, and together with her mate Apsu the fresh water god, she created the original, chaotic world, and ruled it. Tiamat is usually depicted as a monstrous sea-serpent or dragon, and in a battle for the Earth it is Ea who overcomes Apsu, and Marduk who finally slays Tiamat. The result of this victory is to bring order to the chaotic world. Tiamat was the primeval ocean from whence all life sprang, and is known in a variety of forms. The Sumerians knew her as Nammu, who rouses the water-god Enki and together they created mankind.

The Hebrew form of Tiamat is Tohu or Tehom, (the latter being the word for 'waters' in *Genesis*). Another Hebrew goddess is Metsulah, she represents the depths of the sea, and may be linked with Tiamat, as can the Biblical Leviathan (originally a Phoenician sea-monster god).

Quite unlike the sea-serpent goddess Tiamat is the Semitic sea and moon goddess known as Atergatis to the Syrians and Derceto to the Philistines. Atergatis was originally a fertility goddess and probably developed from the Babylonian goddess Ishtar. She eventually became a sea goddess and was widely represented in her mermaid form. As Derceto she is shown as a fish-tailed goddess on a coin struck in Ascalon. In Syria

Atergatis had temples at Hierapolis and Ascalon, and there she had fish proclaimed sacred in her name. As the mermaid, moon goddess Derceto, gold and silver fish were declared sacred and made as offerings. No Syrian would eat fish without the blessing of Atergatis/Derceto herself.

Robert Graves associates Atergatis/Derceto with the Greek moon goddess Artemis and the Cretan goddess Britomart. Fish-tailed statues of Britomart are found in Cephallonia, Crete and elsewhere. Due to the sea-faring nature of her people, the cult of Atergatis reached Egypt and Rome and Spain. There is some evidence to suggest that it even reached British shores.

Derceto was mother to Semiramus, a legendary but fictitious queen of Assyria. When the child Semiramus was born, Derceto tried to kill her, but she was saved and grew to adulthood. In shame of her evil deed Derceto threw herself into a lake and changed the form of her body to that of a fish. Thus Derceto became a mermaid.

In another legend, Derceto is escaping from the attentions of an overly amorous pursuer, (Graves suggests King Moschus). At one point during the chase Derceto changes to fish form. Britomart is found in a similar legend, with King Mines of Crete the pursuer.

If Atergatis/Derceto was the sea-goddess of the early Semitic peoples, then perhaps better known was the fish-tailed sea god of the Philistines, Phoenicians and Syrians. This was Dagon, the merman god. The Old Testament, (Samuel Ch5 V1-14), mentions Dagon. The Philistines had conquered the Israelites and captured the Ark of God, laying it before Dagon's image in their temple to him. The God of the Israelites wrestled with Dagon and overcame him, breaking his statue into pieces and leaving only the stump of his tail. The temple of Dagon where the Philistines laid the Ark of the Covenant was in Ashod. Other temples in his name where found in Gaza. In *TheWhite Goddess* Robert Graves suggests that the Philistines may have been of Cretan origin, despite their Semitic language, and probably brought Dagon with them from the Aegean.

Dagon is generally accepted to have been fish-tailed, although the passage from the Old Testament does not specifically mention this, and only makes reference to the 'stump of a tail' being left after Dagon's statue is brought down. A cylinder seal, dated around 500 BCE shows the god in front of an altar, and here he has the body of a man above the waist and a fish's tail below. Further evidence for Dagon's merman form is that he may be derived fron an older god named Odacon. This god was a form of the Assyro-Babylonian Oannes/Ea, (a theory slightly in conflict with Grave's suggestion of a Mediterranean origin for Dagon). One last indication is that the Hebrew word for a male fish is 'Dag', (a female fish is 'Dagah'.

Classical Greek mythology presents us with many marine gods and goddesses. Archaic Greek culture certainly 'borrowed' from the Babylonians, and remarkable mythological parallels exist, suggesting a large degree of contact between the Greeks and the Semitic peoples of the east. Fish-tailed deities represented in early Greek vase paintings may have been influenced by the Philistine Dagon. Other links in this comparative mythology have been found as far apart as India and Celtic Britain.

Poseidon is probably the best known marine god of the Greeks, but he was not traditionally depicted as fish-tailed. Poseidon drew lots with his brothers Zeus and Hades, and thus received dominion over the seas. He was usually shown in totally human form, riding the waves in a chariot drawn by sea-beasts, or riding a great hippocamp (sea-horse). Poseidon is one of the twelve Olympian Gods, but before his appearance the Greeks had other marine deities.

Pontus (the sea), was the son of Gaia (the Earth) and Uranus (heaven). Together with his mother he produced the sea gods Nereus and Oceanus and the sea goddess Tethys. Nereus was known as 'the Old Man of the Sea', or alternatively 'the

Truthful' and has been represented as fish-tailed. He is, perhaps, better known for being the father of the fifty nereids, sea-nymphs of the coastal waters. Many of the nereids are known by name; 'Speo the Swift', 'Halimede of the Gleaming Diadem', 'Galatea the Beautiful' and 'Amphitrite of the Pretty Ankles'. As the nereids were to the coastal waters, so the oceanids were to the open ocean. The oceanids numbered three thousand, according to Apollodorus the Athenian, and were the children of Tethys and her brother Oceanus. Their unions also produced the naiads of the rivers and springs.

The nereids, (and for that matter the oceanids), were not mermaids in the true sense; they were not fish-tailed. But they did share certain characteristics with the mermaid, although for the most part her more sinister side seems to be absent in the Greek sea-nymphs. The nereids and the oceanids were usually helpful and benevolent. They were beautiful beyond comparison, and lucky the man that glimpsed one. They brought good fortune to those who would treat them with respect, and sailors would invoke them for protection at sea.

The nereids were regarded as minor deities and had their own shrines dotted along the coastline. The singing voice of the nereid was as beautiful and alluring as that of her fish-tailed cousin, but it was not used to lure unwary sailors to their doom. Like the mermaid, the nereids and the oceanids could control the waves, calming as well as raising them. However, for all their benevolence, the Nereids could become vengeful if wronged.

When Cassiopeia, the Queen of Ethiopia, boasted that her daughter Andromeda was more beautiful than the nereids, they took offence and asked Poseidon to punish her. Poseidon sent a sea-monster to devastate the coast of Ethiopia. Cassiopeia's husband was Cepheus, and he decided to sacrifice Andromeda to the monster in the hope that it would stop the monster's terrible rampage. The seemingly doomed girl is, however, rescued at the last minute by the hero Perseus. Cassiopeia must have seriously regretted her act of boastfulness against the nereids.

Amongst the nereids we find Amphitrite, who as a sea-goddess in her own right was loved by Poseidon, and had a son by him, called Triton. More will be told of Triton and his kind later. Another nereid was Thetis, mother of Achilles. Robert Graves describes Thetis as a Thessalonian sea-goddess, and links her with Tethys, the mother of the oceanids.

Although usually represented in human form, we do find a true mermaid goddess amongst the oceanids. The sea-goddess Eurynome (or Euronyme) is represented as fish-tailed at Phigalia in Arcadia (carved in wood). Eurynome was also a moon-goddess, and to the Pelasgians ('sea-farers') she was the great mother-goddess that initiated creation from her union with the cosmic snake Ophion. The Pelasgians claim direct descent from this union.

Eurynome is also linked with two other Greek goddesses. The first is the moon and nature goddess Artemis. Artemis has also been represented in fish-tailed form; a statue in Arcadia shows her as a fish below the waist. At a shrine to her at Iolcus in Southern Thessaly fishermen and sailors took Artemis as their patroness. The name Artemis possibly means 'the disposer of water', but Charles Seltman in *The Twelve Olympians* (1952) suggests that she may have only been a freshwater mermaid, with lakes, rivers, streams and marshes in her care. Both Artemis and Eurynome can be linked to the Cretan goddess Britomart and the fish-tailed Atergatis/ Derceto of the Syrians and Philistines. Already mentioned is the legend of the goddess Derceto taking a fish-tailed form in order to escape an unwanted suitor. This legend is shared by Artemis, Britomart and even Aphrodite who acquires a fish's tail in order to escape the attentions of Apollo the sun-god. The legend goes some way to explaining the fish-tailed forms of these goddesses.

Aphrodite is born from the sea, created when blood from the castrated Uranus mixes with the sea-foam. Aphrodite is the ultimate love-goddess, she is love given form, but her marine origins link her to the ancient sea-goddesses that came before her. Traditionally, Aphrodite came ashore on the coast of Cyprus, and it is here that the sea-faring Phoenicians and Philistines probably introduced her to the Mycenean Greeks, in the guise of their own Astarte and Atergatis. Aphrodite's connection with the sea is undeniable, her symbol is the scallop, itself also representative of a woman's genitals. Temples to her were often built on the coast and sailors would invoke her for protection or sea voyages.

Another goddess associated with Aphrodite is Daeira, said to be the mother of the legendary King Eleusis, and known as 'The Wise One of the Sea'. Daeira is remembered locally on the Balearic island of Majorca as the 'siren' or 'Mermaid'. Small clay whistles called *xiurell* are made for one festival after the harvest to bring a 'winnowing wind' (the wind to blow the chaff from the grain). One traditional shape of the *xiurell* is that of Daeira the mermaid.

Along side the fifty Nereids and the three thousand Oceanids, the seas of Greek mythology were also home to the tritons and their lesser-known mates, the tritonids. Of the tritonids, little is written, but they were fish-tailed, as were the tritons, and both accompanied Poseidon and Amphitrite as they rode the waves. The tritons would swim ahead and blow conch shells to announce the arrival of the god and goddess of the sea.

The tritons are well represented in art; a particularly interesting example is a painting by Eustache Le Seur (1616-1665), showing Poseidon surrounded by Nereids and tritons blowing conch-shells. The whole entourage is shown approaching two sailors, and the presence of cupids flying above suggests the impending mermaid-type marriage of the doomed men to the Nereids. The painting is named 'The Sea-Gods and the God of Love'.

According to Pausanias, writing in the second century A.D., the tritons had the tails of dolphins. They were exuberant and boisterous, not unlike the Irish merrow. In one legend a triton attacks some women of Tanagra while they are swimming, and they are only saved when the god Dionysus hears their cries and overcomes the triton in a fight. The triton of Tanagra was apparently well known for attacking small vessels, but is eventually killed by a local man who finds him sleeping off a drinking binge.

Another legend concerns a fisherman called Glaucus, who is turned into a triton by the sea-deities Oceanus and Tethys. Glaucus the triton had a fish's tail and long flowing green hair.

Although the natural mates for the tritons would seem to have been the tritonids, they often turned their amorous attentions to the Nereids, the Oceanids and to mortal women.

The original Triton was the son of Poseidon and the Nereid Amphitrite. Triton shared the characteristics of his name-sakes and lived in a house of gold at the bottom of the sea. Triton is the first true Greek merman, with a magnificent, spreading tail. In *The Argonautica* Apollonius Rhodios describes him as god-like: '*he was wondrous like the blessed gods in form; but below the loins stretched the tail of a sea-monster, forked this way and that, and with the spines thereof he cleft the surface of the water, for these parted below into two curved fins, like to the horns of the moon*". In *The Argonautica* Triton shows his generous side by offering to guide the Argonauts home. Triton was also famous for his powers of prophesy and his ability to command the waves. He would have undoubtedly been invoked by Greek seamen for his protection during their voyages. Triton is one of the few Greek deities who managed the transition into the Roman mythologies without a name change. Triton accompanied the Roman sea-god, Neptune, in the same way as did Poseidon, blowing a conch-shell before him to herald his father's approach.

Mentioned earlier are the sirens, creatures with singing voices so enchanting that no man could resist the sound. In many places today, a 'siren' is another term for the mermaid, but in their original form the Ancient Greek sirens were half bird, half woman, or woman-faced birds. Homer mentions two sirens who accosted Odysseus, but Robert Graves suggests that they would have originally been a triad, or even an ennead. Sailors passing their island would be lured to their doom by the irresistible singing of the sirens, The seductive song of the mermaid does much the same job, and as the main prey of the sirens were sea-farers, it is not difficult to see how they eventually metamorphosed into mermaid-type creatures. Further evidence for their transformation comes from the fact that the sirens were the daughters of the river god Achelous, who was sometimes depicted as a merman himself.

The mother of the sirens was one of the Muses, but classical scholars cannot seem to agree on which one. Early depictions of the siren by Greek artists show her in her bird-woman form. The transformation from bird-woman to fish-tailed mermaid was gradual, and began in the Hellenistic period. The seductive singing voice was retained and by the Middle Ages the 'siren' had become a mermaid. Interestingly, transitional forms of the siren appear in many of the early bestiaries. Illustrations of 'syrens' with fish tails, but also feathers and the talons of a bird of prey are relatively common. Similar composite creatures are also found carved in churches.

An interesting footnote is worth a mention here. A transitional siren/mermaid was reported from Exmouth in Devon in 1812. A Mr. Toupin of that town claims to have seen a mermaid with feathers on her neck, back and loins. Mr. Toupin also claims to have heard the creature singing; one wonders, in this case, how he survived to tell the tale!

Certainly the siren of Ancient Greece can be considered an ancestor of the mermaid, at least as much as any sea-goddess can.

Throughout the world the mythologies of countless peoples include fish- tailed deities. In North America a tradition of the Shawano people tells of a fish-tailed man that arose from the waters of a great salt lake. Although the man rode through the waters on the back of a great fish, he had the tail of a fish himself. The man's face was shaped like that of a porpoise and he had green hair like seaweed. About his neck was a magnificent string of sea-shells and he carried a whale-bone staff. When the man spoke to the Shawano in their own language, they were terrified.

The man-fish continued to appear to the people, and although they were still frightened, they would gather on the shore of the great salt lake to hear his beautiful singing voice. The man-fish also taught the people many things and they suspected that he was a god. Although they feared his strange appearance, they eventually grew accustomed to him and put their fear aside. The Shawano would sit before the man-fish, who sat with his twin fish-tails coiled beneath him, and they would listen as he told them tales of beautiful things in the ocean and of a wonderful land of plenty beyond the salt lake. The man-fish offered to lead the Shawano, and guide them across the water to this land where he said they would prosper. At first the people were afraid to follow him, but eventually things started to go badly for them and they began te starve. Starvation overcame fear, and they agreed to follow the man-fish with his promises of plenty.

The people set off in their canoes and travelled across the water, braving storms and huge waves, but all the time following the man-fish who swam before them and urged them on. After two moons and a half, the Shawano came to a green shore. They were cold, wet and very hungry, and glad to have come to the end of their journey. The land they had reached was lush with vegetation and alive with game, the whole place was bathed in brilliant sunlight and the sun warmed their hearts as well as their bodies. True to his word, the man-fish had led the people to a promised land.

The story continues, what is related above is only a part, and it tells of the eventual settlement of the Shawano on the western banks of the Mississippi The man-fish was not seen again by the people, but from then on they prospered as he had promised. The man-fish of the Shawano shows marked similarities with the Babylonian Oannes in his role as bringer of wisdom and civilisation to his people.

Further north the mythology of the Haidah people of British Columbia includes the powerful merman god Tchimose. Like the man-fish of the Shawano, Tchimose had twin fish tails, but unlike him, Tchimose was greatly feared for his destructive malevolence. The mythology of the Inuit contains, not surprisingly, many sea-dwelling deities and spirits. Chief amongst these is the sea-goddess Sedna (or Anaknagak). Sedna has power over animals, and can prevent them from providing themselves as food for the people if she is not properly propitiated. Sedna will also raise storms if she is unhappy, and is usually depicted as huge and one-eyed. Other Inuit sea-deities include Aipalookvik, an evil god or spirit, responsible for destroying boats and fishermen, and Aulanerk who is generally regarded as beneficent, even though his underwater struggles cause large waves.

Descended from the oldest African sea-gods and goddesses, are the merman and mermaid deities of the powerful voodoo religions of the Caribbean and Brazil. The Haitian voodoo goddess Erzulie is a triple goddess originating in Dahome (or Benin). In her maiden form, Erzulie is associated with the sea, and like Aphrodite is also a goddess of love. Erzulie is called 'La Sirene' in this form and is the wife of the powerful Haitian sea-god, Agwe. 'La Sirene' is blue in colour and her voice is said to hiss like the sea.

Descended from the mythology of the Nigerian Yoruba people is Yemaja (or Yemanja), Yemaja is the 'fish-mother' and an important goddess in Brazilian Voodoo. As her name suggests, her dominion is over the sea, lakes and rivers. Yemaja came across the Atlantic with the African slave trade, and evolved into the supreme Voodoo mother goddess. She was the daughter of the Earth Goddess Odudua and gave birth herself to eleven other gods and goddesses, as well as the moon and the sun. Yemaja is often depicted as a mermaid goddess and has links with the Christian virgin Mary. Offerings to her were left at the shoreline every New Year's Eve.

The coastal dwelling Yoruba of Nigeria also worship the husband of Yemaja, the sea-god Olokun. Olokun is said to live in a magnificent palace beneath the sea and has mermaids and mermen as servants. A 14th century king of Benin once claimed to be an incarnation of Olokun, and he said that he had acquired the tail of a mud fish instead of his legs. The reasoning behind the king's claim was one of survival. An incomplete or imperfect man could not be king (as with Celtic culture), and should a king become imperfect in any way, he would be put to death. The miraculous deification of this particular king was due to gradual deterioration and eventual paralysis of his legs. His claim to be the fish-tailed sea-god (which prevented him being able to walk on land), saved not only his kingship but also his life. Luckily for the king, his newly acquired tail was sacred and had to be kept covered at all times.

Already mentioned is the Hindu god Matsya, the first avatar, or incarnation of Vishnu; Matsya is portrayed as a great horned fish, or fish-tailed deity "blazing with gold", at the time of the Hindu deluge. In this form Vishni slays a demon and recovers the sacred Vedas, stolen by the demon. Matsya then abates the waters.

The River Ganges, the greatest of the sacred Hindu rivers, was ruled by the water goddess Ganga. Ganga is usually depicted as a beautiful young woman surrounded by flowing water, and she descends to Earth as seven streams, so as not to cause a catastrophe. Where the Ganges leaves the Himalayas is a pool, sacred in Hindu lore, at Hardwar. Hindu pilgrims feed sacred salmon that lived in the pool. This brings to mind the Irish myth of the sacred pool, attended by priestesses, at the source of the River Boyne. 'The Salmon of Knowledge' was said to live in the pool, and the priestesses would feed it hazel nuts from nine sacred trees.

In China the sea-goddess T'ien Hou is also known as the 'Empress of Heaven'. She is the protectress of sailors and fishermen, (and nowadays even lifeboat crews), and gives warning of approaching storms, a characteristic common-lyattributed to mermaids. T'ien Hou is widely worshipped in her homeland, and this worship has spread to Hong Kong and the Chinese communities of California.

From E.T.C. Werner's *Myths and Legends of China* (1922), Benwell and Waugh relate the myths of the Chinese Dragon-Kings and their wives. There were five Dragon-Kings, one relating to each of the four cardinal points and the fifth at the centre. The Dragon-Kings lived under the sea in wondrous, transparent palaces, attended by their numerous offspring.

A Chinese creator goddess called Nu-Kua is described as a beautiful woman from the waist up, but with a huge dragon's tail below. The legend goes, that Nu-Kua created men and women, intending to model them on herself, but changed her mind and gave them legs instead of a tail. Like the Babylonian Ea/Oannes, Nu-Kua is attributed with teaching human-kind the civilised sciences, including irrigation.

The Japanese have similar legends of the Dragon-Kings, and the sea-king Rinjin (or Ryujin) is a dragon-god. Rinjin lives in a many storeyed palace under the sea, built from red and white coral. The palace is guarded by colourful dragons, and within, time passes differently to the outside world. A day in the sea-king's palace is the same as one hundred years on Earth.

Beyond China and Japan lies the world's largest ocean; the Pacific. From this massive area comes a wealth of mermaid folklore and mythology. Some Pacific mermaid and merman deities have already been mentioned in the previous chapter, but there are many more worth a mention.

The Javanese Ocean Goddess goes under a variety of names. She is the personification of the Pacific, called Nyai Loro Kidul or Nyai Belorong. As Ratu Loro Kidul she is the 'Virgin Queen of the Southern Ocean', and is the goddess of rain and storms. Nyai Loro Kidul has retained her position, even amongst the Muslim Javanese, and people sometimes sleep on the beach in order to obtain revelations from her. She is said to live in a magnificent palace under the sea, (an obvious and common dwelling place of marine deities), and holds court here, attended by her mermaid and merman servants. Among her attendants is Jin Laut, a malevolent sea-demon, and her servant Kyai Belorong.

Kyai Belorong is fish-tailed and has one thousand arms and legs. He is covered with golden scales and has his own mermaid servants to wait on him. He also has his own palace, with a roof of human skeletons and pillars of living men (actually those who have drowned at sea). It is said that any man can take as much of Kyai Belorong's gold as he can carry, but must die after seven years if he does.

Fishermen throughout the Pacific region would pray to their respective sea deities, offering sacrifices in some cases, such as those made to Ratu Loro Kidul by the Javanese. In the Aru Islands a gong is dropped into the sea as an offering to the sea-god Taidue. Great lengths are gone to, to ensure that the sea-god Waruna of the Balinese is properly propitiated. Waruna is God of the Ocean and of the rains.

Already mentioned is Tangaroa, the creator fish-god of the Polynesian peoples, (known in an almost identical form to the Hawaiians and Tongans as Tangalba). Tangaroa gives birth to all the sea creatures, including the mer-folk, who themselves eventually 'evolve' into human beings. Tangaroa is, in effect,

Nyai Loro kidul - Ocean Goddess

the Polynesian Poseidon, and is so huge that he only needs to breath twice in every tqenty-four hours. The breathing of the sea-god creates the tidal flow.

Also from the Polynesian island group is the sea-goddess Hina-Ika, ('Lady of the Fish'). The husband of Hina-Ika is Ira-Waru, an ancient fish-god in merman form. Local belief was that women swimming too far from the shore ran the risk of male fish mating with them, thus creating mer-folk offspring in the image of Ira-Waru.

An interesting merman deity in Thai mythology is Machanu, the guardian of a great lake that must be crossed in order to reach the underworld, (called Patal in Thai, after the Sanskrit Patala). The concept of sea-deities also being those of the underworld, or the passage to it, is not uncommon. The Chaldean goddess Sabitu has her palace on the sea-shore of the ocean that encircles the world, she is goddess of the underworld as well the 'Waters of Death' before it. Another Chaldean goddess, Siduri, plays a similar role. In both these cases the sea is the symbol of the feminine intuitive aspect.

It is obviously well beyond the scope of this book to explore all the water deities of the world, let alone those that can be associated with the origins of the mer-folk and other water-spirits. A few interesting examples from around the world have been given. True, not all are fish-tailed, and there are as many gods as there are goddesses, but all are the distant ancestors of the mermaid and her mate. The mermaid inherits her attributes and character from them all; her roles as the raiser of storms, controller of the waves and collector of drowned souls are all those of the sea-deities of old. Her appearance as fish-tailed woman is as necessary as it is obvious.

Water can be as deadly an element as it is vital for life. The sea can be unpredictable and uncontrollable, changing its nature in an instant. The water-deities were, not surprisingly, powerful and important, and it is also not surprising that, even with the advent of Christianity, people were loathe to reject them totally. Echoes of the belief in them remain all around us, even today, and they even became associated with Christian saints in some cases. The gods and goddesses of watery places have diminished into the water-sprites, the nymphs and the undines and, most ancient of all, the mermaids

Chapter 4

The Mermaid and the Christian Church

The mermaid may be descended from the most ancient sea-goddesses but, in Western Europe at least, with the advent of Christianity, she gradually developed a peculiar relationship with the Church. This relationship seemed to reach a peak in the Middle Ages, and her image, both carved and painted was common in both church and cathedral alike.

In their work *The Sea Enchantress* Benwell and Waugh list many examples of mer-folk imagery in churches, the results of their exhaustive research. Doubtless many church carvings of mermaids would have been lost due to the activities of Puritan iconoclasts, but plenty seem to have survived.

The church stone-masons and craftsmen depicted many fantastic and mythological creatures, alongside the more traditional biblical and domestic subjects. The mermaid was certainly not alone, and shared the churches with dragons griffins, gargoyles and others, including the 'green man' foliate heads. Along with the green man she seems to have been a particular favourite of the craftsmen, appearing in a variety of poses and forms. Transitional 'siren' type creatures were also sometimes depicted, complete with feathers or wings and a fish's tail.

So where did these Mediaeval craftsmen place her? It is common to find the mermaid carved on misericords, (the hinged seats in a choir stall). The carving would usually be made on the underside of the seat, for obvious reasons! Pews and bench-ends where often elaborately decorated with animals, figures

Chalice - Woman's association with water

and scenes, and the mermaid appears here in many churches. Elsewhere she can be found on roof bosses and corbels, (the boss is a projection placed to hide the unsightly joins of ribs or groins and the corbel is a projection on the face of a wall, used to support the ribs). Occasionally the mermaid appears elsewhere, such as on cornices, doors, tympanums, and on rare occasions she encircles the font either alone or with her mate.

The mermaid carved in the fifteenth century on a bench-end in Zennor church has already been mentioned, and the folk-tale connected to this carving is told later. The Zennor mermaid is shown in traditional pose with comb and mirror, and this pose is repeated many times in church carvings. Examples are to be found on a corbel at Hereford Cathedral and on a misericord in the Henry VII chapel of Westminster Abbey. The parish church of St. Margaret at Kilkhampton has 157 beautifully carved oak bench-ends; one has three mermaids, each with comb and mirror, on a heraldic shield. At St. Oswald's in Malpas, Cheshire, a mermaid with her traditional possessions is carved on a misericord.

On occasion the mermaid is shown grasping a fish instead of a comb or mirror. In examples of this kind, the fish symbolises the Christian faith itself, and the mermaid is the pagan sea-goddess attempting to ensnare the souls of the faithful. In certain Mediaeval mystery plays a mermaid is used to represent the duality of Christ as part man, part divine. A mermaid with a fish is found on a misericord in Beverly Minster, Yorkshire and one is carved in the Chapel of St. Paul at Exeter Cathedral. Mermaids were sometimes shown grasping their own tails, or their plaited hair. A roof boss in the 14th century church of St. Nectan at Hartland in Devon, has a mermaid holding her tail in her left hand. Interestingly she is not as old as the church, but is the work of a 20th century craftsman, who carved her as part of the church's restoration. Another mermaid grasping her own tail is to be found carved on a boss in Exeter Cathedral Presbytery.

The mermaid is often associated with other, real and mythological, creatures in a heraldic style. She is carved with dolphin supporters at Norwich Cathedral, Gloucester Cathedral and at Ludlow. Strangely, she is also sometimes depicted suckling a heraldic lion, (again at Norwich and also at Wells Cathedral). Benwell and Waugh speculate that this representation may be linked to the goddess Artemis (who has a mermaid form), and who is herself sometimes shown with lions. Artemis is shown on a vase found in Boetia with her arms extended above two lions. On her close-fitting robe a fish symbol is shown. Also represented in church carvings are mermaids playing musical instruments, perhaps as an accompaniment to their irresistible singing voice.

Also, but rarely, mermaids are shown with their mermen mates. A wall painting in Raaby church, Jutland shows both merman and mermaid. Both are carved on misericords at All Saints, Hereford and St. Mary's, Stratford-on-Avon. Mermen are sometimes shown on their own, such as those encircling the font at St. Peter's in Cambridge.

The mermaid is sometimes painted in murals, usually alongside St. Christopher, the patron saint of travellers. St. Christopher examples survive at St. Breaca's in Breage, Cornwall, St. Jame's in Bramley, Hampshire and at St. Olaf's in Poughill, Cornwall.

So why is such a pagan creature, descendant of the sea-goddesses and water-cults, so frequently represented in Christian places of worship?

Certainly the Mediaeval craftsmen would have known her well. They undoubtedly took inspiration from the bestiaries of the time; this much is evident, simply from the way she is usually shown by the craftsmen. Also, at the time these same craftsmen were carving (and painting) her, she was firmly believed in as a real creature. And this belief was not just restricted to the common people; the Church endorsed the belief by allowing the representation of mermaids, as well as many other fabulous creatures. Sailors, bringing back tales of marvels seen at sea and in far off lands, added weight to the general acceptance of creatures we know to be merely mythological today.

Many of the bestiaries were written by churchmen, monks or clerics in Holy Orders. The 'Syren' or mermaid featured alongside real creatures, as well as other mythological 'oddities' believed to be real at the time. Mediaeval bestiaries would have originally been compiled in Latin, and completely beyond the mostly illiterate laity. Pictures and carvings were used by the Church te get around this, and get their messages across. Written, as they were, with the hand of the Church, the bestiaries were often moralist in nature, as well as claiming to be complete descriptions of the natural history of the world. Often creatures were described in terms of their character or nature in relation to Christian ideals.

The work *De Propietatibus rerum* was the encyclopedic 'mastpiece' written in the 13th century by Bartholomew Angelicus. As well as writings on the sciences and geography, Bartholomew describes plants and animals, including the mermaid, who he tells us "are strong whores, that drew men that passed by them, into poverty and mischief......". Bartholomew goes on to accuse the 'siren', (as he calls her), of ravishing men after she has lulled them to sleep with her singing, and then killing and eating them.

In the 12th century work *The Hortus Deliciarum,* the Abbess of Mont Saint-Odile deals similarly with the Greek sirens and uses their attack on Odysseus as a a moralistic tale. The sirens represent the seductions of the world, with Odysseus himself standing for the Christian world.

So what was the message the church wanted their congregations to learn through the image of the mermaid?

Liban

In many folk-tales the mermaid is depicted as a wanton, immoral creature. Her sole purpose in life was to lure men into sin and any man so ensnared was punished with death or some equally terrible fate. In fact the message frrom the Church was little more than an indirect attack on the ancient sea-goddess herself, whose temptations must be resisted. It was more obviously a thinly veiled attack on women, with their failings, sinful tendencies and an inability to control their voracious sexual appetites! Throughout the journey of life, decent and righteous men would certainly be confronted with almost irresistible temptations, usually of a sexual nature. In the same way sailors were drawn to a watery grave by the song of the mermaid. Forewarned with knowledge of the peril, a good Christian man could resist the sins of thf flesh, as Odysseus had resisted the song of the siren, and Christianity could be seen to triumph over the pagan.

Inevitably the influence of the Christian Church spread to the folklore and legend of the mermaid. The story of the mermaid Liban told in an earlier chapter is a 'Christianised' version of a much older tale. The story tells of Liban's encounter with St. Comgall. In an Irish legend, another saint, St. Patrick, actually transforms some women into mermaids. The story goes that these were old pagan women who harassed the saint as he passed them by. St. Patrick transforms the women into mermaids as a punishment and banishes them from the earth, "thus adding to the perils of the sea". St. Patrick also encounters the merman, Fintan, and is instrumental in his conversion to Christianity. Fintan came to Ireland before the flood, and survived the deluge, when it came, by changing into a fish. After his conversion by St. Patrick, Fintan was himself canonized.

A mermaid once visited the shores of Iona and implored a monk to grant her salvation and a place in heaven. Daily she visited the monk with her plea, but was only ever given the answer that she must forswear the sea forever. Despite the mermaid's longing for a soul, the call of the sea was too great to resist. She made one last desperate plea to the monk, but he remained adamant, and she disappeared forever into her watery realm.

The mermaid desperate for a soul in the last tale was said to have visited Iona in 563CE. As Christianity grew in strength throughout Europe this theme is found more and more in folk and fairy-tales; it is commonly found in tales about mermaids and other water-spirits. The moral to the tale is that, in order to obtain salvation, the pagan must completely give up the old heathen ways and embrace the god of the Christians. Fair enough. It would seem to be a reasonable thing to expect. In the mermaid's case however, it would seem to be an almost impossible requirement.

Many European folk-tales involve a water-spirit of some kind imploring Christian holy man for a soul. This type of moralist tale was especially popular by the Middle Ages. The Mediaeval mermaid, it would seem, was continually in torment; tortured by her desperate need for the forgiveness of the Christian God, and for entrance into heaven. Her inability to completely give up the sea will inevitably deny her final salvation, and she is condemned to a 'life' wandering the cold oceans.

Having said this, it was not always the case. Liban is given the choice of dying immediately and ascending to heaven or staying on earth as long as she has lived in the sea. Liban chooses to die immediately and is baptised by St. Comgall so that she may enter heaven. From then on, Liban is counted as one of the Holy Virgins.

Harsher treatment of a Scottish mermaid leads her to plunge, shrieking, into the sea. The mermaid in question, "a beautiful green lady of the sea" meets a man reading his Bible on the shore. The mermaid enquires about her chances of salvation according to the holy book, and is told in no uncertain terms that she does not stand a chance! This unwelcome news is the cause of the mermaid's distressed and and noisy exit.

The dangers of attempting to interfere on behalf of a mermaid are made clear in the tale of the man that tried to save the soul of his recently deceased mermaid wife. The man has his wife's body buried in the local churchyard, but the mermaid's forsaken kins-folk are heard wailing and moaning from a nearby creek. One morning a great tidal bore floods the land and engulfs the church with the congregation inside. The graves around the churchyard, including that of the mermaid wife, are opened up by the flood water, and give up their dead. The mer-folk are waiting in the creek, and receive the mermaid wife's body. They bare her away to the sea.

The Scandinavian water-spirit (The Nack in Sweden and the Nokk in Norway) also longs for salvation, and has been known to include this in his price for teaching mortal men to play the fiddle. From *The Fairy Mythology* by Thomas Keightly (1850) comes the tale of a Swedish nack that meets with two young boys that are playing by the river. The boys spy the nack as he is playing his harp, and inform the water-spirit that there will be no place for him in heaven. This revelation distresses the poor nack so much that he flings away his harp and, weeping bitterly, sinks beneath the water. The children return home and tell their father of their meeting with the nack. The father, who happens to be the local priest, is shocked at the boys' behaviour and sends them straight back to the river to tell the nack that he may be saved. The boys return and find the distraught nack playing a mournful lament on his harp. They tell him that he may find a place in heaven, and that his soul can be saved. The nack is overjoyed and plays happily on his harp until the sun goes down.

A similar tale, also from Sweden, concerns a priest with a far less forgiving nature. This particular priest tells a nack that his walking staff is more likely to take root and sprout leaves and flowers, than he is to enter heaven.

The priest, obviously pleased with himself at putting the pagan creature in its place, sets off down the road. The nack is left to

Bench end carving - Zennor church, Cornwall

bemoan his lot, but the priest has not gone very far when, to his astonishment, his staff sets down roots and sprouts leaves and flowers. To the priest this is obviously a miracle and a sign, and remembering what he has told the nack, he turns around and hurries back to the creature. The priest tells the nack of the miracle, and its obvious implication. Salvation is indeed possible for the nack after all, and he is so happy that he plays sweetly on his harp for the whole night.

The Merman of Nissum, a tale from Denmark, tells of a merman buried in consecrated ground in Nissum churchyard. In this curious tale a merman is washed up dead and found by the local people. The people bury the merman in the churchyard, but as soon as the burial is over a strange wind picks up and blows sand inland from the dunes and beach. The sand covers the town and countryside, and the people consult a local wiseman, who immediately knew that the dead merman was to blame. The wiseman tells the worried towns-folk to disinter the merman, and look to see how far he has sucked his forefinger into his mouth. If the merman has sucked the finger past the second joint then all is lost and nothing can be done, but if he has not yet sucked it that far, then there was a chance to save the town. This was done, and the people saw that he had not yet sucked his finger past the second joint. The wiseman advised the people to quickly bury the merman in the dunes, and when this was done, the strange wind dropped and Nissum was saved.

It would seem that simply burying a merman in consecrated ground can bring down a curse. Obviously the merman buried at Nissum did not receive final salvation, despite the local people allowing him a place in their churchyard. Perhaps not all the mer-folk were so interested in obtaining a Christian soul after all!

A mermaid was taken in Holland in 1403 after a violent storm had washed away many dykes. The mermaid was washed up near the town of Edam, and taken to Harlem, where she lived on land for fifteen years with a pious mistress. The mermaid was taught to bow before the crucifix, and she obeyed her mistress without question, but in all her fifteen years on land she never uttered a single word. When the mermaid died, she was granted burial in the local churchyard, but in this case there is no record of any misfortune occurring. The mermaid's conversion had obviously been complete, and no doubt she was able to enter heaven.

In a tale from the Faeroes, told later, a merman captured by the fisherman Anfinn is held captive by the sign of the cross being made over him. The first time Anfinn forgets to make the sign, the merman escapes. The tale demonstrates the influence of Christianity; the pagan merman is defeated by the power of Christianity, but constant vigilance was needed to keep paganism subdued.

Another tale told later describes a mermaid being frightened by the utterance of a holy oath, (although in another version of the same tale she is offended by swearing). C.S. Burne in her *Shropshire Folk-lore* (1883) prefers the idea that the mention of the holy name effectively 'exorcizes' the pagan mermaid.

It also seems that holy water can sometimes be effective in repelling mermaids. 'Sirens', (as mermaids are sometimes called in France), once inhabited a bay near La Rochelle, where they would amuse themselves by luring fishermen and then spiriting them away. Fed up with losing their men to these licentious creatures, the local women got together and swam out to the sirens' favourite rock. Each woman carried with her a bottle of holy water, which they smashed on the rock. The sirens, "with their big cold eyes", screamed and dived into the sea, never to return. Not long after, the bodies of all the men they had lured away were washed up on the beach.

The mermaid's apparent fear of Christianity, and her power-lessness before it, brings to mind the tale of St. Columba, and his encounter with another type of water-spirit. Columba is accredited with bringing Christianity to the pagan Picts, and in a show of power he defeats a kelpie simply by naming his god, and making the sign of the cross before it. This, of course, is St. Columba's famous encounter with the Loch Ness Monster. In the story, the 'monster' or kelpie is terrified by the saint's words, and retreats back into the inky depths of the loch.

The early Christian missionaries were well aware of the power of the pagan water-cults in Britain and Europe. Over time the Church made it its business to absorb the sacred wells, fountains and lakes, making them holy places, and effectively putting down the attendant water-spirit. Such places were dedicated to god and the saints, but perhaps of all the pagan cults, those associated with water lingered the longest. Christian Franks continued to make sacrifices to the River Po. 'Pagan-style' rituals still occur at some holy wells in the Celtic countries, such as the tying of 'clouties', (strips of cloth), near Madron well in Cornwall to rid oneself of ailments.

Despite the bad press levelled at her by the Christian Church, the mermaid survived, in fact her image today is much improved. Just as the Church used the skill and art of the craftsmen to show the mermaid as an immoral and wanton pagan temptress, other artists were inspired by the beauty and romance of the mermaid and her folk-lore. The mermaid is well represented in art, poetry and literature and it is to this subject we turn next.

Chapter 5

The Mermaid in Art and Literature

Down through the ages countless artists, poets and writers have taken the mermaid as their inspiration. In her guise as a elemental water-spirit she is, after all, representative of creative intuition. It is the element of water that inspires the artist within us to paint pictures, create poetry or compose music.

Possibly the earliest known depiction of a fish-tailed human figure is a sculpture from Assyria showing the merman god Oannes. The sculpture is now safely housed in the Louvre and is nearly three thousand years old. The ancient Greeks painted mermaids on vases the Amerindians carved and painted her on cliffs. In Medieval Europe she appeared in illustrated bestiaries, in heraldry and as an embellishment on maps.

But in Europe at least, the mermaid as artist's subject reached a peak in the romantic art of the 19th century. Many of the better-known mermaid images that we see today on cards and posters come from this period. The way in which mermaids were depicted varied somewhat and seemed to depend on the disposition of the particular artist, and she tended to be painted from two different stand points. The mermaid was either shown as a gentle beauty combing her long hair or playing happily in the waves. Or else she was painted as the treacherous femme fatale of the sea, luring helpless sea-men to their doom. In this way it seems that her representation in art mirrors that of her folklore.

I started an earlier chapter with a description of John William Waterhouse's beautiful painting, *A Mermaid*. Waterhouse's mermaid certainly falls into the former of these two categories. As well as 'A Mermaid' painted in 1901 for the R.A Summer Exhibition he produced other works along a similar theme. A study for 'A Mermaid', and a beautiful picture in its own right, was painted in 1892 and foreshadowed the 1901 work, and in 1900 Waterhouse painted ghe Siren' in which a mermaid holding a lyre sits on a rock and gazes sadly down at a drowning sailor. The mermaid has drawn the sailor to his doom. but mourns for her victim. 'The Siren' obviously tends towards the latter of the two categories, but lacks any hint of violence, only sadness. Another work by Waterhouse is worth a mention here, a piece probably better known than either 'A Mermaid' or 'The Siren', and painted in 1896. 'Hylas and the Nymphs' is probably the most widely exhibited of Waterhouse's paintings, and possibly only second to 'The Lady of Shalott' in fame. The painting shows the enchantment of the youth Hylas by water-nymphs who have risen from a lily-covered pool.

Waterhouse was a follower of the Pre-Raphaelites, and mostly painted romantic figures, often from myth and legend. Victorian England was consumed with sexual inhibition and neuroses. Painting mythological beauties, be they mermaid or otherwise, gave the artists of the time a means to depict the naked or semi-naked form without risking the wrath of the academic art world. Continuing this "classical" theme; the mermaid's victim in many paintings from this period was usually a handsome youth or hero-like figure. Seldom, if ever, did the victim look like a typical fisherman or sailor.

One painting from the Victorian era that is an exception to the above rule, is Howard Pyle's mermaid and pirate. The pair are engaged in a passionate kiss, and although the painting was never published it has, nevertheless, become well known.

The Neoclassicists Edward Burne-Jones and Frederick Leighton both took the legendary mermaid as a subject for a painting. Leighton's painting 'The Fisherman and the Siren' is based around a poem by Goethe. The mermaid has her arms clasped around a fisherman's neck, in the way a lover might, and she kisses him passionately, head tilted back and breasts pressed against his body. The picture is sensuous and erotic, but on further examination it seems that the fisherman is in fact a helpless victim. His arms are outstretched and he is powerless to resist. It becomes clear that the mermaid will eventually drag him down and drown him.

Leighton's mermaid has long flowing red/brown hair and, interestingly, her tail starts low down, her human buttocks are clearly visible, adding to the sexual nature of the subject. 19th century artists often depicted mermaids in this way. Burne-Jones does so in 'The Siren' and Waterhouse's 'Siren' has a tail that starts well below the knees. In Burne-Jon's painting there is no ambiguity about the fate of the mermaid's victim. Burne-Jones shows him already submerged, being dragged down through the water by the mermaid who has her arms clasped tight around his waist. No lover's embrace here!

As mentioned above, Howard Pyle's mermaid is engaged in a passionate kiss with a pirate. This beautiful picture is painted in tones of sea-green and blue. The pirate's red cap is evocative of the 'cohuleen druith', the magical red cap of the Irish mermaids (the merrows). The cohuleen druith allows the wearer to move through the water unhindered, and works equally well for mermaid or human. One has to wonder whether the pirate is in luck here, Maybe his mermaid lover has given him the magical cap to keep him safe in her world.

Edvard Munch is best known for his brooding and sometimes disturbing paintings, his most famous painting, 'The Scream' is a prime example. Munch also painted a siren-like figure, a vampiric 'bird-woman' standing astride her victim, and a mermaid painting by the artist has a somewhat sinister quality. Munch's mermaid also has a tail that starts low down, her human genitals are visible, as are her breasts. Again, sexual

92

imagery is implied, but the eerie stare of the red-haired mermaid should be enough to warn off any potential human lover.

Herbert Draper takes the legend of Odysseus and the Sirens as the inspiration for a beautiful painting. The Ancient Greeks depicted scenes from the legends themselves, with the sirens in their traditional bird-women form. Draper chooses to show one of the sirens as a mermaid, although another is completely tailless and closer to a nereid or sea-nymph of some kind. As in the legend, Odysseus is shown tied to the mast of his ship, so that he might hear the song of the sirens, but resists their lure and his doom.

Waterhouse painted his own version of the Siren legend in 1891. In Waterhouse's picture the hero Ulysses and the sirens are in their more traditional form, with the heads of women on the bodies of birds of prey. Ulysses is tied to the mast of his ship, as Odyssues is in Draper's painting. The scene is dramatic, with the circle of predatory sirens concentrating their attention on the hero.

The Swiss artist Arnold Brocklin also produced mermaid paintings in the 19th century. 'Playing in the Waves' painted in the early 1880's shows a mermaid and merman, 'Games of Naiads' painted in 1886 shows mermaids at play and the picture 'Calm Sea' from the same year shows a mermaid with bright red hair lounging on a rock, while her mate gazes at her from the water.

Mermaids also inspired several paintings by one of the greatest fairy artists of the late 19th and early 20th centuries. Arthur Rackham illustrated fairy tales and literary classics, such as *Peter Pan* and *A Midsummer Night's Dream*. From the latter is a beautiful mermaid painting "...certain stars shot madly from their spheres to hear the sea-maid's music". Rackham produced the piece in 1908, and it shows the 'sea-maid sitting on the back of a great fish, (or Whale?), combing her long flowing hair.

Waves curl high behind her and the sea is churning in typical Rackham style. In the middle of the bottom border is a medallion of Queen Elizabeth I.

Interestingly, Elizabeth's 'enemy', Mary Queen of Scots was once portrayed as a mermaid. Nearly 350 years before Rackham's painting, a cartoon of Mary appeared in the 1567 *Scottish Calender of State Papers* after her defeat at Carberry Hill. The illustration shows the ill-fated Mary with a fish's tail and holding a curious 'winged staff'.

Also, some Shakespearian scholars claim that the passage in *A Midsummer Night's Dream* that refers to the mermaid, or sea-maid is actually a veiled reference to Mary. One assumes that Rackham may have known this and had the relationship between Elizabeth and Mary in mind when illustrating the passage.

> *"Thou rememb'rest*
> *Since once I sat upon a promontory,*
> *And heard a mermaid on a dolphin's back*
> *Uttering such dulcet and harmonious breath,*
> *That the rude sea grew civil at her song,*
> *And certain stars shot madly from their spheres,*
> *To hear the sea-maid's music."*

Arthur Rackham produced another mermaid painting in 1909, called 'Jewels from the Deep'. The painting shows two mermaids offering a shell full of precious jewels to a youth who has dived into the water. The youth's companions await him in their boat, which itself is a giant scallop shell. In the same year Rackham also produced a painting called 'Undine Outside the Window', which he later stated was a particular favourite of his. Rackham was illustrating the book *Undine* by Friedrich de la Motte Fouque at the time, a story of a water-nymph who loved a knight. 'Undine' is described later in this chapter.

Of course, mermaids have featured in art right up to the present day. Many artists have taken her as their inspiration, and she features strongly in fantasy art, one of the most popular art-forms of the late 20th century. In 1948 Rene Magritte painted an interesting variation on the theme. 'Song of Love' shows a reversal of the mermaid form, with the heads of fish on human bodies. Artists such as Andrew Loomis in the 50's and Boris Vallejo in the 70's created more traditional mermaid art. 'Fish Girl' by Chris Achilleos is a slightly less traditional, but nevertheless beautiful example. The painting shows a mermaid with the body and fins of a lion fish.

In literature the mermaid is probably best commemorated in Hans Christiar Anderson's tragic love story, *The Little Mermaid*. Since the animated Disney version of the story *The Little Mermaid* has been reintroduced to a whole new generation of children and parents.

Anderson's tale is well known and has many elements common to mermaid folklore. It is a tale of unrequited love and tragedy, of sacrifice and the longing for a Christian soul. The little mermaid falls in love with a human from the "countries above the sea", a Prince whom she saves from drowning after his ship is wrecked by a storm. The little mermaid makes a deal with a sea-witch and gains legs instead of a fish-tail, so that she might go on land and search for her prince. But there is a price. For the little mermaid to walk on land as a human, she must suffer agonies as if she were walking on knife blades and sharp pins. And possibly worse still, she must trade her beautiful voice for the human legs and so become mute.

The little mermaid suffers her agonies gladly for the chance to be with her prince, but trading her voice brings her nothing but misfortune. She finds her prince, but can never tell him how she feels, or that she is the one who saved his life. Although he grows fond of her, he loves another and marries a princess from a neighbouring country. Once this happens the little mermaid knows she is doomed to die, for the prince can never be hers.

Her sisters, whe have also bargained with the sea-witch, appear and try to save her. They have sold their hair to the sea-witch for a magic knife, with which the little mermaid must kill the prince and so be returned to her fish-tailed form. Sadly this can never be, she loves the prince too much and cannot kill him. She dies in the first rays of the sun after the wedding night.

The tale is set very much in the Christian world. The little mermaid longs for an immortal soul, so that she may enter the kingdom of God. When she dies, her body dissolves to sea-foam, and her spirit joins those of the air. This is the fate of all mermaids who die. The only way for the little mermaid to get a soul is for her to gain the unconditional love of a human man. Once joined in a Christian marriage by a priest, that man's own soul would flow into her, making her truly human. Thus the little mermaid is condemned to join the elementals of the air. In time she may enter heaven, but each time a child is bad she must shed tears for that child. Each tear adds a day to her existence as a spirit of the air.

In Shakespeare's day certain women at court would sometimes be called 'mermaids'. The term was a derogatory one, and was aimed at those women thought to barter sexual favours for the purposes of social climbing. The portrayal of Mary Queen of Scots as a cartoon mermaid was probably drawn with this intention. Shakespeare himself mentions 'a mermaid' in this derogatory sense in *A Comedy of Errors*. Antipholus addresses Luciana:

> "O, train me not, sweet mermaid, with thy note
> To drown me in thy sister's flow of tears,
> Sing, siren, for thyself, and I will dote:
> Spread o'er the silver waves thy golden hairs,
> And as a bed I'll take them, and there lie;
> And in that glorious supposition, think
> He gains by death that hath such means to die;
> Let Love, being light, be drowned if she sink!"

Shakespeare's reference to a mermaid, or 'sea-maid', in *A Midsummer Night's Dream* has been mentioned. He also makes reference to mermaids in *Hamlet, Antony and Cleopatra* and *Troy Depicted*. In Shakespeare's time the famous Mermaid Tavern in Bread Street, Cheapside was the meeting place of a literary club. Shakespeare would meet here with the likes of Ben Jonson and Christopher Marlowe to exchange witty banter. Marlowe also alludes to mermaids in his *Hero and Leander*.

> *"Leander strived; the waves about him wound,*
> *And pulled him to the bottom, where the ground*
> *Was strewed with pearl, and in low coral groves*
> *Sweet singing mermaids sported with their loves*
> *On heaps of heavy gold, and took great pleasure*
> *To spurn in careless sport the shipwreck treasure."*

Today the Mermaid in Bread Street has gone, but The Mermaid Theatre, often host to the plays of Shakespeare, stands near to the original site.

A young writer called William Diaper published *The Nereides: or Sea-Eclogues* in 1712. The eclogues are dialogues, some between nereids and tritons. The triton Glaucus is accused by a nereid named Cymothoe of favouring another over her, an accusation that Glaucus vehemently denies. Diaper came to the notice of society due to the recommendations of Jonathan Swift.

In the 19th century Roden Wriothesley Noel wrote *The Water-Nymph and the Boy* in which a mermaid or water-nymph haunts a pool in some woods. The water nymph drowns a boy in her pool and justifies her actions to his grief stricken parents, saying that she has saved him from the ravages of old age. The water nymph thinks that this is explanation enough and cannot comprehend the parents' inability to understand her reasoning.

The mermaid's mate is celebrated in the poem *The Forsaken Merman* by Matthew Arnold. The merman takes a human bride, Margaret, and she lives with him under the sea. Margaret and the merman live happily with their children, until one day she hears the bells of a church on land, and longs to return there to attend the sermon.

"She said: "I must go, for my kinsfolk pray
In the little grey church on the shore today.
'Twill be Easter-time in the world - ah me!
And I lose my poor soul, Merman, here with thee."

Margaret returns to land, and her merman mate is forsaken. He tries to win her back by getting the children to call to their mother, but it is to no avail Margaret, in fear for her soul, has rediscovered Christianity and will not return.

"But, ah! she gave me never a look,
For her eyes were seal'd to the holy book"

Margaret does miss her family under the sea, but never returns. The merman eventually accepts that he has lost her forever, and has the painful task of explaining the loss to his children. All they can do is look upon the town where their mother lives, and then return to the depths of the sea.

"We will gaze from the sand-hills
At the white, sleeping town,
At the church on the hillside,..
And then come back down"

Friedrich de la motte Fouque wrote the romance *Undine* in 1811. In the tale an old fisherman and his wife lose their young daughter in a terrible storm but at the same time a beautiful infant is washed up near their house. They adopt the child to replace their own, but as the child grows, she insists that her name is Undine and feels strangely drawn to water. The old fisherman and his wife love her deeply, but worry about her strange, 'un-Christian' behaviour.

Meanwhile, the couple's real daughter, who had not drowned as they had feared, was being reared as a princess by a duke and duchess. The duke and duchess call her Bertalda, and one day she charges a handsome knight to retrieve her glove from a dark and sinister forest. The knight enters the forest, which is near the old fisherman's house, and there, comes across Undine playing near a lake. The knight immediately falls in love with Undine, and takes her back as: his wife, even though she has explained that she is a water-nymph, and has no Christian soul. The act of marriage to the knight will grant her salvation.

In the meantime, Bertalda has discovered that her true parents are really only poor fisher-folk, and not royalty. Undine loves Bertalda like a sister and takes her in at her knight's castle. Unfortunately the knight has grown suspicious of Undine's supernatural nature, and his love slowly turns to the completely human Bertalda. Added to this, Undine's true kinsfolk, the sea nymphs are determined to get her back.

In an attempt to thwart her kinsfolk, Undine stresses to the knight that he must never curse her if they are on open water. If he does she will be lost to him forever. Unfortunately the knight forgets one day when they are at sea during a storm. Undine disappears into the waves, and the knight returns alone to the castle and Bertalda. The knight soon dies, and Undine appears at his funeral as a white water-wraith. When the knight is buried, she dissolves into a fountain.

Other water-spirits appear in story, poem and ballad. One of the seal-folk, or silkies, is represented in the Shetland Isles ballad *The Great Silkie of Sule Skerry*. There are several versions of the ballad, which tells of a mortal girl who has a child by a silkie, one of the seal-folk. The girl is unaware of her lover's true identity at the time, but he tells her who he is and makes a prophesy that he and their son will one day be killed by a "proud gunner" who she will eventually marry. The prophesy unfortunately comes true, the girl marries a man who finally shoots the silkie and the son she had by him.

The Nibelungenlied is the Iliad of the Germanic people, and was written in about 1200 AD by an anonymous poet. The water-sprites or nixes (wasser-nixen) appear to Hagen on the banks of The River Danube, as he is about to cross over and enter the land of the Huns. The nixes give a prophetic warning to Hagen; death lays across the waters of the river for him and all his knights. The vision holds true and with the death of Hagen, the last of the Nibelung lords is gone, and the treasure of the Nibelung disappears forever from the sight of men.

Mermaids also appear in traditional ballads from time to time, and in a few she is the main character. *The Mermaid* is a 19th century ballad from the Ayrshire coast in Scotland that appears in a number of collections. The mermaid in question succeeds in luring a knight to his doom, and is most definitely depicted as the villain of the piece. The folk-tale *McPhie and the Mermaid*, (told later), is converted into ballad in *The Mermaid of Colonsay*. In the ballad, by John Leyden, McPhie becomes Macphail and, like McPhie, is imprisoned in a cave for seven months by the mermaid. Macphail eventually tricks her and escapes.

The mermaid is an excellent subject for any romantic tale tinged with tragedy. Modern writers continue to be inspired by her. Of course the huge amount of mermaid folklore is also literature, and it is to the folk-tales of the mer-folk that we will turn to next.

Chapter 6
The Mermaid in Folklore

Almost every country has its own water-spirit folklore. We find them in the lakes, rivers and pools, in the wells and springs, and of course in the sea. The widespread nature of mermaid lore, and its apparent antiquity, is testament to man's fascination, fear and love of the sea. Her story is that of uncanny beauty, irresistible temptation, undying love, betrayal and death. 'Folklore' means just that; the traditional beliefs and tales of a people or race, and can include the true beliefs of the people, that could be called 'legends', and the more fanciful 'fairy-tales' of oral storytellers, created for entertainment.

Within the latter, however, are often still traceable the strands of ancient folk tradition and belief systems. An important distinction, based on distribution, exists in folklore. Folk-tales generally can be classed as 'local' or 'migratory', and this holds true for mermaid lore. The same basic folk-tale plot may be found in a number of different versions. With a fine tuning of details to suit a particular setting or characteristic regional variant, the tale develops. These are the migratory tales, and core themes or 'motifs' are often found in several different countries. An example of the migratory tale, spread in the early Christian era, is the 'fairie's prospect of salvation'. As described earlier, examples of this kind are certainly found in mermaid folklore. True local tales are not found anywhere but the place of their origin.

The same themes occur again and again in different folk tales. An example of this from British mermaid lore is found in the tales *Lutey and the Mermaid* and *The Old Man of Cury*. Both stories are from Cornwall and contain the theme or motif of a grateful mermaid rewarding a man who helps her back to the sea. The setting and outcome of the tales are different, but the two stories are basically one and the same. Another commonly found theme is the 'fairy bride' type. In these tales the union is always doomed to fail. Katherine Briggs writes, in her *A Dictionary of Fairies* (1976) "..*the ends of all these intercourses between immortality and mortality have been tragic*".

Tales of mermaids luring, or attempting to lure, men into the sea, are also common. In British, Irish and Northern European folklore a great many themes exist, and some of the more common ones will be seen in the examples that follow. Often the themes are easy to pick out, but sometimes more than one may exist within a single story and this hints at the way the folklore has developed over many years. This can happen as the stories migrate and are interchanged. Truly 'local' folk-tales are harder to pin down, but some are more obvious than others. *The Mermaid of Marden* is an unusual tale and may be considered 'local'.

For a detailed account of folk-tale motifs and their classification the reader should turn to Katherine Brigg's *A Dictionary of British Folk Tales in the English Language*, Part B, (1970), or the older *Types of the Folktale* (1910), written by Antti Aarne, and revised by Professor Stith Thompson.

What follows is a selection of tales, mainly from Britain and Europe, of the mermaid and her kin. A few examples from around the world will be related in context, but it is safe to say that the mermaid lore of the British Isles alone would fill a book many times the size of this one.

Index of Folk-tales

The Mermaid's Vengeance (Selina)
The Padstow Doombar
The Child's Ercall Mermaid
The Mermaid of Aqualate Mere
The Mermaid of Marden

Wales
The Sea-Kina's Daughter (Nefvn)
Pergrin and the Mermaid
The Conway Mermaid
St.Patrick's Encounter
The Lady of Llyn Y Fan Fach

Isle of Man
The Mermaid Mist
The Spurned Mermaid
'Egg Water'
The Wren Hunt Legend

Ireland
The Soul Cages
Dick Fitgerald and the Mermaid
Shea and the Mermaid's Curse
The Mermaid and the Butler
Blind Maurice

Scotland
The Jealous Mermaid
MacPhie and the Mermaid
The Mermaid's Knots
The Mermaid and the Baby Seals
John Reid and the Mermaid
The Mermaid of Knockdolian
The Blue Men of the Minch

Shetland and Orkney
"Skoom well your fish"
The Washing Mermaid of Loch Sin

The Goodman of Wastness
The Mermaid and the Selkie
The Wounded Seal-Father
Gioga and Ollavitinus
The Kelpie's Name

Scandinavia, Denmark and Iceland
The Green Giant - Denmark
The Mermaid's Cattle - Denmark
The Merman's Rock - Denmark
The Wise Merman - Iceland
Anfinn and the Merman - Faeroes
"Better the skin than the child" - Iceland
"The hour has come but not the man" - Norway
The Dancers Who Could Not Stop - Sweden
The Water-Horse - Denmark

Europe
The Lorelei - Germany
Melusine - France, Germany, Italy, Estonia, Luxembourg
Brauherd's Mermaid - Germany

Elsewhere
The Mermaid and the Farmer - Japan
The Rujung - Japan
The Sea-King's Daughter - China
The Tears of the Samebito - Indonesia
The Pascagoula and the Mermaid - USA (Louisiana)
The Fish-Man - Canada (British Columbia)

Chapter 7

The Folklore of Mermaids and Other Water-Spirits

England, Wales and The Isle of Man

In England the mermaid and her kin would seem to favour the coastline of Cornwall. Cornwall has a coastline 300 miles long, often rugged and wild, and you are never more than 15 miles from the sea at any point in the county. It is understandable that the sea and a sea-faring way of life played a huge part in the lives of the local people, and so did maritime superstitions and folklore.

The name of the old Cornish sea-god has been forgotten, but elements of this possibly live on in fairy lore. Margaret Courtney, in her *Cornish Feasts and Folklore* (1890), makes reference to the 'Bucca', a spirit that fishermen felt it necessary to propitiate by leaving three fish from the catch on the sands. This practice was necessary to ensure future catches and was still evident at the turn of the century. Dr. W.Y. Evan-Wentz, in his *Fairy-Faith in Celtic Countries* (1911) states that Bucca is properly a deity, or the descendant of one, and not a fairy at all. Whether the Bucca was fish-tailed is not stated, but he is described as having 'fishy eyes and hair like seaweed'.

In Cornwall mermaids were often referred to as 'merry-maids' or 'meremaids' Descriptions were usually of classic mermaid type and behaviour. Possibly the most famous Cornish mermaid is the, previously mentioned, Mermaid of Zennor whose image can still be seen today carved on a pew-end in Zennor church.

A Cornish Mermaid

A mermaid was once drawn from the sea at Zennor by the beautiful singing voice of a chorister named Matthew Trewhella. She would sit quietly in the church and listen to Matthew sing, and the local parishioners wondered at who the beautiful stranger might be, but her identity remained a mystery. Eventually the mermaid managed to lure the unfortunate Matthew into the sea and spirited him away to sing for her alone in her ocean home. Matthew was never seen again, but local legend has it that Matthew's singing can still be heard in Pendour Cove from beneath the waves.

An interesting sequel to this story appears later on. A mermaid once appeared in the water at the side of a ship anchored in Pendour Cove and complained to the captain that his anchor was blocking the entrance to her underwater home. The mermaid added that she shared her home with one Mathy Trewhella.

On the south coast of West Penwith is the beautiful Lamorna Cove. A rock offshore here is known locally as 'The Mermaid's Rock'. A mermaid appears on the rock, singing as the precursor of a storm or a wreck. Her singing is also said to have lured many young men to drown as they swim, mesmerised, out to the rock, and are never seen again.

The Lamorna mermaid is obviously an example of a malevolent creature, but the one that a Cornishman named Lutey happened across seemed more friendly. Lutey came across a mermaid who had apparently been stranded by the tide. The mermaid begged Lutey to help her back to the ocean before her merman husband discovered her absence and devoured their children. Lutey agreed (horrified at the possible plight of the mer-children), and for his trouble the mermaid made him a gift of her golden comb. She told Lutey that if he ever needed her help he was to comb the water three times and call her name, which was Morvenna (sea woman). The generous Morvenna also granted Lutey three wishes, which being a selfless man, he chose the power to break the spells of witchcraft; power over spirits in order to protect others from them; and the continuation of these gifts to his descendents.

These gifts the mermaid granted, but taking a shine to the lad, she did try and persuade him into the sea with her. Lutey refused, happy with life on land and faithful to his wife. Disappointed, the mermaid swam off but called back to Lutey that she would come for him after nine years was up.

Morvenna was true to her word, and after nine years she appeared to Lutey while he was out fishing with a friend. Lutey seems to have been resigned to his fate and said simply "My hour is come " before plunging into the depths with the mermaid and disappering forever.

It is said that Lutey's descendents continued to become powerful white witches, the famous 'pellars' of the Lizard peninsula, but that every nine years one or more were claimed by the sea.

Lutey and the Mermaid is taken from William Bottrell's *Traditions and Hearthside Stories of West Cornwall* (1870). A similar story is related by Robert Hunt in his *Popular Romances of the West of England* (1881), but in *The Old Man of Cury* the old man is not claimed by the mermaid and lives out his life, passing on the gifts granted by the mermaid to his family.

Robert Hunt also relates the tragic tale of *The Mermaid's Vengeance*. This story is unusual in that, although mermaids are quick to avenge harm done to themselves and their kin, the vengeance in question is taken on behalf of a human girl named Selina. The story is commonly set in Perranzabuloe, but is found in Perranporth and a few other places along the Cornish coast.

As a child, Selina, the daughter of Penna and Honour, visited a pool near the rocks of Perran with her parents. This pool was a haunt of mermaids, and during the visit Selina suddenly became excited, and to her mother's horror she leapt into the water and disappeared. The child quickly reappeared however, but was strangely different; radiant and more beautiful than she had been before. Other changes became apparent in the days that followed, Selina loved to dance, but now hated entering the church. Some old wise women advised Selina's parents that the child was a changeling and not their daughter at all.

Selina grew from a beautiful child into a beautiful woman, and at the age of eighteen met Walter Trewoofe, a soldier and son of the local squire. At this time also, an enemy of Selina's father named Tom Chenalls tricked him into leaving the family home to work on a farm at Land's End. With her father away, Walter Trewoofe took advantage of the young Selina, and having got her pregnant, took off for the city. The betrayed girl carried the child, but pined away, and in her weakened state she died in childbirth.

Walter Trewoofe eventually returned home to live, and one night in a drunken state, he was staggering along the beach when to his surprise a woman, the exact likeness of the dead Selina, met him at the mouth of a cave. The woman was in truth a mermaid who had taken the child Selina under her protection and was out to avenge her betrayal and death. The drunken Trewoofe was easily fooled and, thinking this to be Selina, took her in his arms. Suddenly a terrible storm arose and the mermaid's grip became vice-like. Try as he might Trewoofe could not get free, and so was dragged into the sea by the vengeful mermaid, where he was drowned.

Mermaids taking vengeance for wrongs done to themselves form the basis of other Cornish tales. A mermaid who frequented Padstow harbour was shot at one day and vowed on the spot to make the harbour unusable and desolate. The mermaid formed a great sand-bar (the Doom Bar) that choked the harbour with sand and caused many ships to go aground.

At Seaton near Looe on the south coast of Cornwall a mermaid was injured by a sailor. Local legend says that in retaliation she caused the town to be overwhelmed with sand, until eventually it dwindled from a flourishing coastal town to little more than a few houses and a small sandy beach.

Procreation between mer-folk and humans seems to be a common motif in folklore and in places that have a strong mermaid mythology mermaid or merman ancestry is often claimed. Cornwall is no exception and several families claim to be descended from the mer-folk. Members of such families were thought to possess various powers beyond the ordinary as part of their legacy. Sometimes it was said that their children were born with evidence of webbing between their fingers.

Elsewhere in England mermaid legends are relatively rare. However, unlike some other types of 'sea fairy', mermaids seem to be quite at home in fresh water, and in some English legends this is where we find her.

At Childs Ercall in Shropshire a pond once harboured a solitary mermaid. A story tells of two men passing the pond early one morning on their way to do a day's work. As they neared the water the men spotted something odd on the surface, which they soon realised was the mermaid. The mermaid frightened the men so much that they made to flee, but at that point she spoke to them in a voice so sweet that it rooted them to the spot. More than this, both men fell instantly in love with her. The mermaid told the men that a great treasure lay at the bottom of the pond and she would fetch it to them on one condition they must come into the water and take the gold from her hands. Both men, hopelessly in love and eager to obtain the gold, waded in almost up to ther chins, whereupon the mermaid dived down and returned with a huge lump of gold which she held out for them to take. In his excitement at the sight of so much gold, one of the men suddenly cried out an oath. The mermaid gave a shriek snatched back the gold and dived down, never to be seen again.

Whether the man swore and offended the mermaid, or uttered a holy oath and so frightened such a pagan creature is a matter for speculation.

Another Shropshire mermaid lived in Aqualate Mere. When an attempt was made to drain the mere she appeared on the surface and threatened to flood the nearby towns of Newport and Meretown.

E.M Leather in *Folk-Lore of Herefordshire* tells the peculiar tale of the *Mermaid of Marden*. A long time ago the church at Marden used to be nearer the river than it is today, and one day due to a misfortune, one of the church bells ended up in the river and was immediately seized by a mermaid who lived there. The mermaid dived down to the bottom of the river with the stolen bell and held it fast there. The parishioners consulted a local wise-man about how to recover the bell from the adamant mermaid, and he told them. A team of twelve white heifers must be attached to the bell with yokes of sacred yew held together with bands of mountain ash. The bell was to be drawn out in perfect silence so as not to awaken the mermaid who would now be asleep. This was successfully done, and the bell brought up to the edge of the river. But on seeing the mermaid curled up, asleep, inside the bell the team driver completely forgot the advice of the wise-man and let out a cry. The mermaid awoke suddenly, and seeing that she was being tricked, grabbed the bell and plunged back into the river, this time for good. Local legend says that the bell lies at the bottom of a deep clear pool and can sometimes be heard ringing.

Another fresh water mermaid haunts the Mermaid's Pool at Chapel-en-le-Frith in Derbyshire. Local legend says that if a person stares into the depths of the pool at midnight on Easter Day eve, they might catch a glimpse of its beautiful inhabitant. Also, any man who has the luck to see her bathing will have the gift of immortality bestowed upon him by the mermaid.

Wales

The Welsh surname Morgan means 'born of the sea'. It is also a Welsh term for the mermaid and is probably related to the Breton morgen, or Nari Morgen (daughter who sings amid the sea).

Wales has less mermaid folklore than one would expect from a country with such a wild and beautiful coastline and a rich tradition of story tellers and bards, but those that we do find here are classics of their kind.

In the Cornish tale of 'Lutey and the Mermaid' the mermaid is named Morvenna, meaning 'sea-woman'. A Welsh tale tells of the sea-king's daughter, the mermaid Nefyn. A fisherman named Ifan Morgan found the mermaid Nefyn in a coastal cave one day, but she begged him to leave her be and return the next day. That night Nefyn ate most of the fish in the nets nearby and so when Ifan returned the next day he was astonished to find a transformation had taken place.

The mermaid now had the appearance of a finely gowned lady. Nefyn handed Ifan a cap and confessed her love for him, and so they married and she bore the man five pairs of twins. As they grew, the children grew suspicious of their mother's true nature. She could calm storms at sea with a word, and so one night the eldest son followed her down to the shore. The son watched in horror as his mother threw a mantle over herself and his father and then the pair leapt into the sea together and disappeared.

The eldest son now knew that his mother was a mermaid and was so heart-broken that he died of grief. The boy's coffin was taken to the shore, that one of his mother's people might claim his body and take it into the ocean. No sooner had the first wave touched the coffin than the boy leapt out. Then a ship appeared from nowhere and he boarded it. The ship and the eldest son of Nefyn and Ifan disappeared to the sound of strange and wonderful music. As if this wasn't enough, the eldest daughter of Nefyn and Ifan threw herself into the sea after hher brother, crazed with grief as she was. A sea-knight met the girl and carried her away also.

Later, when Ifan Morgan died, the mermaid Nefyn returned to her true home and was not seen on land again.

Other places on the Welsh coast lay claim to mermaids. St. Dogmael's, near Cardigan is the setting for a tale in which a mermaid gives a warning. One day whilst fishing, a man named Pergrin caught a mermaid that he had spied sitting on a rock. Once aboard his boat, the mermaid begged for Pergrin to release her, and said that if he did she would come to his aid three times. Pergrin was not a bad man and on the mermaid's promise he released her to the sea. Some time later the boats were out on a calm sea when the mermaid suddenly appeared by the side of Pergrin's boat and bade him take up his nets and make urgently for the shore. Pergrin did so without question, but as the sea was calm no other boats followed his and continued to fish. Pergrin and his men made it home just as a fierce storm blew up out of nowhere, but the boats that had stayed to fish were lost with all hands.

Pergrin released the mermaid and was rewarded for his mercy, but when the people of Conway refused to free a mermaid they had captured she died and cursed them. It is said that the people of Conway remain poor as a result.

Inland in Wales we find tales of the Gwragedd Annwn, water-fairies of the lakes. It is said that they were long-lived, beautiful and benevolent, and like the mermaids, would often take mortal husbands and bear them children. Wirt Sikes in *British Goblins* (1880) says that several old Welsh families claim to be descended from them.

A story goes that St. Patrick was over from Ireland visiting St. David and the pair were walking by the side of Crumlym Lake, when St. Patrick was abused by some local women. The women were harassing Patrick for deserting his native Wales for Erin, and he caused the women to be cast into the lake and transformed into fish. Later he relented slightly and left them as water fairies, the Gwragedd Annwn. A similar legend involving the saint is found in Ireland. Here St. Patrick turns some old pagan women into mermaids, and so banishes them from the earth.

Sir John Rhys in his *Celtic Folklore* (1901) gives a version of the story of the *Lady of Llyn y Fan Fach*, taken from Rees of Tonn's introduction to *The Physicians of Mydfai'*(1861). The Lady in question is a member of the Gwragede Annwn and the story has elements of a typical mermaid/fairy marriage type folk-tale.

Llyn y Fan Fach is a beautiful lake near the Black Mountains. A widow lived at a farm nearby at Blaensawde and one day she sent her only son to graze cattle in the valley near the lake. The young man sat down to eat his lunch on the shores of the lake and saw a beautiful woman on the surface of the water, combing her long golden hair. She was using the still surface of the lake as her mirror, and was the most lovely woman he had ever seen. At that moment he fell deeply and hopelessly in love.

The young man proclaimed his love to the woman and beseeched her to come to the shore. Twice she declined, but on the third occasion she agreed. The young man proposed marriage, and gained permission from the fairy woman's father who gave her a dowry of as many cattle as she could count in a breath. But as with many marriages to members of the fairy race there was to be a proviso; if the man should strike her three causeless blows during their marriage, it would come to an end and she would return to the lake. The young man quickly agreed, never imagining for one second that this would ever happen.

The union was a happy one and, in time, the fairy woman had three sons. But as with many fairy folk, the woman had some strange habits. She would weep at a wedding and laugh gaily and sing at a funeral. This behaviour embarrassed her husband on several occasions and led to one, two then a third reproachful tap on his wife's arm. The instant the third tap was done the fairy woman took her dowry cattle and returned to the lake. Her husband never saw her again.

The fairy woman did not forget her sons however, and would appear to them at the lake side, where she taught them the secrets of medicine. The three sons became the famous physicians of Mydfai, and their skills were passed down to their descendants.

Isle of Man.

The Isle of Man is popularly said to be named after Manannan mac Lir, the Danannan god of the sea more commonly associated with Ireland. The Manx name for the mermaid is the 'Ben-Varrey' and the merman is the 'Doinney-Varrey'. The island is rich in mermaid lore.

The Isle of Man is frequently covered in a dense mist, causing problems in days past for shipping that could all too easily end up wrecked on her rocky coastline. A folk-tale of Man blames a mermaid's curse for these mists, yet another tale of a mermaid's vengeance after being wronged by a man. In this case it is not down to a physical assault on the mermaid, but rather by hurt pride.

One day a mermaid that had surfaced saw a handsome man on the beach before her, and fell instantly in love with him. This love she made known to the man in no uncertain terms, but the man, surprised at her sudden appearance and form reacted with horror. The mermaid was insulted and hurt, and took her vengeance by bringing an impenetrable mist down on the island to punish the man and all his kind.

In a similar story George Waldron, in his *Description of the Isle of Man* (1744), tells how a mermaid falls in love with a handsome young man she sees tending his sheep on the shore. When the mermaid throws her arms around him, the man, fearing she means to drag him into the sea, struggles free and runs away. The mermaid, who was simply trying to show him the true nature of her love, is hurt so deeply that in her anger she throws a stone at the fleeing man, which finds its mark. The young man is afflicted soon after with agonising pains and dies within a week. The mermaid is never seen again.

Waldron also relates the following story. According to Manx legend mermaids were frequently seen offshore, cavorting in the sea or sitting about combing their long hair, and on occasion islanders would try and capture one. One night some men succeeded and took a mermaid in their nets. She was beautiful to look at, the perfect appearance of a lovely woman from the waist up, but with the tail of a fish below. The mermaid was taken to the house of one of her captors, and although they treated her well, they could not get her to take food or water, nor speak a word. After a few days the wretched creature began to look very ill. The men, fearing she would die, (and presumably frightened of the consequences if she did), returned her to the sea. Once the mermaid entered the water the men saw a great many other mermaids swim up to greet her. From their vantage point the men heard one of the mermaids ask her what she had learned from the land people, and her answer surprised them. She had learned nothing much at all, except that the land people were so very ignorant as to throw away the water in which they boiled eggs. What the mysterious properties of egg water are, she did not say.

A peculiar piece of folklore to find associated with a mermaid is connected to the barbaric custom of the Christmas-tide wren hunt. The practice of the hunting, killing and displaying of the wren continued in the Isle of Man until well into the nineteenth century (although the custom continued into the early twentieth century without a wren actually being killed. The bird was replaced by a garland of vegetation). In the folklore of the island a mermaid (or fairy in another version) would lure men into the sea by virtue of an irresistible singing voice and then drown them. After suffering for many years from this peril the islanders took the advice of a wise knight who laid a trap for the mermaid. The trap was mostly successful (although what it entailed is not explained), but the mermaid did escape at the last moment by turning into a wren.

The custom of hunting the wren was, according to William Jones in his *Credulities Past and Present* (1880) "was to extirpate the mermaid or fairy: lest she should return to her evil practice". The body of the wren was paraded around, wings outstretched, on a pole and money was given to the successful hunters. Afterwards the feathers would be carefully preserved and used as protection from shipwrecks in the year to come. In the Celtic world the wren is a sacred bird, and killing it was considered taboo, or in more recent times, very bad luck at least. In the general reversion of 'misrule' practised around the Christmas festival this taboo is dropped and, for one day only, the poor bird was ritually killed. The hunt was commonly held on Christmas Day in Manx custom, but St. Stephen's Day (Boxing Day) was more common in Wales and Ireland

Chapter 8

Ireland, Scotland and the Islands

Ireland

Ireland has a strong tradition of mermaid folklore, and has many names for both mermaids and mermen. These include the 'suire', the bamghubba' and the 'murdhuacha' (pronounced muroo-cha) or 'morvadh'. The latter has been Anglicized somewhat to 'merrow' and this is now the most common term used for the Irish sea-folk.

In Irish folklore we also come across a typical mermaid characteristic; this magical item needed to enable the merrow to live in the sea. This item is often described as a magic cap (the *cohuleen druith*) or sometimes as a feather worn in the hair. The colour of cap or feather is usually red and without it the merrow is helplessly trapped on land until it is recovered.

The female merrow has the same basic appearance as the mermaid; a beautiful woman with long flowing tresses (often green), lovely dark eyes and a fish's tail. The male however has a terrifying appearance; green skin, green hair and sharp green teeth, a pointed red nose and small piggy eyes. He is described as being very ugly indeed, but for all his ugliness the male merrow has a friendly and jovial character, as will be seen in the tale of the Soul Cages from County Clare.

The best known and most excellent examples of Irish mermaid lore come from Thomas Crofton Croker in his *Fairy Legends and Traditions of the South of Ireland*, published in 1825. Crofton Croker travelled through Ireland collecting stories

118

directly from the local people and made a record of tales only transmitted previously by an oral tradition. His work *Fairy Legends...* is of immense value, as the tales bear the hallmark of genuine folklore.

The Soul Cages is related by Crofton Croker in volume II of 'Fairy Legends... and tells of Jack Dogherty, a County Clare fisherman who longed to see a merrow. Jack lived with his wife in a small cottage by the sea and longed to one day make the acquaintance of a merrow as his grandfather had done. Day after day, as he went about his business, Jack looked in vain for the tell-tale signs that a merrow was about, the splash of a fin or a flash of the red cap under the waves. One day he finally spotted what looked like such a creature sitting on a rock. The rock was about half a mile out from the shore and, as he drew closer, Jack could see the red of the cohuleen druith perched on the merrow's head. To Jack's dismay, and before he could get close enough to speak to the creature, it dived into the sea and was gone.

Now Jack had seen the merrow he had always wanted to see, but this was not enough; having clapped eyes on the creature he wanted more. Jack was taunted by the knowledge that his grandfather had been great friends with a male merrow and he wanted to earn the merrow's friendship himself as the old man had done.

Jack ventured out to the merrow's rock time and again, and sometimes caught tantalising glimpses of the creature as it played about in the breakers. Then on one particularly stormy day, Jack got right up close and he was treated to a perfect view of the ugly fellow. To Jack's surprise the merrow turned to look at him and hailed him by name.

"Good day to you, Jack Dogherty, how have you been keeping?" Jack was shocked and asked the merrow how it knew his name.

The Merrow

"And why wouldn't I know your name?" the merrow replied, "I was like a brother to your own grandfather."

This merrow and the one his grandfather had known were one and the same, and Jack became its friend as the old man had done before him.

One day the pair met at the rock and Jack saw that the merrow had a spare cap exactly the same as the one he wore himself.

"Would you care to borrow my second cap and visit my wine cellar Jack?" the merrow asked.

Jack feared he would drown if he went with the merrow and voiced his fears.

"Then you are not a quarter the man your grandfather was, he never stood a minute when the chance was offered him."

This taunt encouraged Jack and he took the cap and put it on. The merrow told him to hold onto his tail and then dived down deep into the ocean with Jack in tow. Down and down they went, Jack not daring to try and breath, even though he wore the cohuleen druith, until with a bump the journey ended and he found himself in air again. Jack looked up and saw the bottom of the ocean above as if it was the sky, he could see fish swimming in it as if they were birds. Before him lay the merrow's house, normal in all respects with even smoke curling up from the chimney.

The merrow invited Jack inside and together they ate a good meal of all kinds of fish. The merrow was free with the wine from his cellar and before long seemed drunk and boisterous. He told Jack that his name was Coomara and invited him to see his collection of treasures recovered from the sea. Jack marvelled at the curiosities the merrow had collected over the years, but was puzzled by a great row of wicker lobster pots lined up in rows.

"Why do you keep those Coomara?" Jack asked.

"Those are the soul cages," said Coomara. "Within them are the souls of fishermen and sailors drowned. I scatter the pots around on the bottom during a storm, and any souls that come down, cold and lost, creep inside them for warmth, and there they stay."

Jack was shocked, but never said a word. He listened hard and fancied that he could hear a low, soft sound, like a sob, from any pot he put his ear to, and the sound disturbed him. Jack thought that Coomara meant well, giving the souls a haven, but the thought of them being trapped like lobsters made him sad.

The time came for Jack to return and the merrow shoved him up through the sea. Once at the surface Jack threw the merrow's spare cap back down as he had been asked and went home. The soul cages haunted his thoughts for a long time, and in the end Jack resolved to free the souls and send them on their way to salvation. Jack decided to get Coomara drunk and free the souls then. He wanted to keep his new friend and would get the merrow drunk enough not to realise that it had been he that had released them.

The time came, when his wife was away, and Jack went to Coomara's rock to invite the merrow to his house on the shore. The pair got to drinking and as time went on Jack passed out in a drunken stupor. When he awoke, with a huge headache, Coomara had gone home, having drunk Jack under the table. Jack was quite downcast, his plan had failed and he was at a loss. Luckily his wife would be away for at least a week, as she had gone on a pilgrimage, and so Jack went back out to the rock and invited Coomara back, challenging him to a return drinking match the next day. Coomara could not resist and agreed readily.

122

Jack had one last hope. He had a keg of potcheen stashed away and this he would get out for their match, hoping that the merrow would not be as used to this as he obviously was with whiskey, brandy and rum.

Coomara came to Jack's house the next day, keen to defeat his friend in their drinking match, and Jack met him with the potcheen keg at the ready.

"I've kept this till last," he explained, "It's a keg of real potcheen, very special and hard to come by."

Coomara and Jack began their drinking, but for each drink the pair took, Jack watered his own without the merrow knowing. It was not long before Jack had drunk Coomara under the table, and he ripped the magic cap off the merrow's head and set off for the sea as fast as he could. Jack reached the house under the sea and took up as many of the soul cages as he could carry. Jack took them out of the house and turned them up. The faintest flicker of light shot up from each upturned basket, and Jack thought that he heard a quiet whistle as each soul was freed. Quickly he returned to the house and removed the rest of the soul cages, upturning each one, until at last all were done. Jack said a blessing after the souls to speed them on their way and then put the empty baskets back as he had found them and made ready to return to the surface. Without Coomara to shove him up Jack had trouble getting into the sea above him, but just then a cod dipped its tail down into the air and quick as a flash Jack grabbed it and was carried back up through the water.

Back at his house Jack found Coomara still asleep, and returned the magic cap as if nothing had happened. When he did finally awake, Coomara was so ashamed to have been out-drunk that he sneaked off back to the sea, none the wiser.

Jack and the merrow stayed good friends for many years, and often Jack would make some excuse to go down, and free any new souls that had been caught. One day Jack went out to the rock and threw his stone, but Coomara never came. Jack didn't know what to make of this, the merrow was a mere youngster for his kind, and couldn't have died on him. Jack surmised that maybe Coomara had simply gone away without explanation to live in another part of the sea. Jack longed to go and check for himself, but the merrow still had the spare cap, and Jack was stuck.

Although he visited the rock and often threw his stone in, Coomara never came. Jack had seen the last of his friend, the merrow.

Crofton Croker tells another folk-tale involving the cohuleen druith set near the small village of Gollerus in the south of Ireland. A local man named Dick Fitzgerald saw a mermaid one day, as she sat on a rock combing her long hair. The mermaid's magic cap, that enabled her to move freely in the waters of the ocean, lay on the sand where she had casually dropped it. Now Dick knew that without the little cap the mermaid would be unable to return to the water, and quick as a flash he seized it. The mermaid wept and begged Dick to return her cap, but Dick refused, and finally persuaded the mermaid to be his wife.

The mermaid was an excellent wife and bore Dick three children, but for all her begging, the cap was denied her all this time. Dick knew that she would return to the sea as soon as she got it, leaving him and their childrer behind. Dick hid the cap from his wife, but one day he had to go to Tralee, leaving her and the children at home. The mermaid went about her wifely duties after he was gone, but when she moved Dick's fishing tackle to clean, she found a hole in the wall, and inside it was her cap.

The mermaid was deliriously happy with her discovery, but hesitated before putting the cap on, for she knew the consequences. If she returned to the sea she would never see her children again. But the lure of her ocean home was too great and she put the cap on and went down to the shore. Saying farewell to her three children, she dived in and was never seen again.

Dick returned and found his wife gone. He quickly realised what had happened and fell into despair. Dick mourned his wife's loss for years and waited in vain for her return, but she never came back.

In Ireland we also find tales of vengeful mermaids that have been wronged, and a few tales of lake mermaids. Of the former is a story about a fisherman named Shea who killed a mermaid. Even in death the mermaid was a dangerous creature, and when Shea sailed his fishing boat the day after the evil deed, the sea rose in fury against him and an 'avenging wave' overtook him as he made for the shore in his guilty terror. Shea was drowned, but the mermaid, not content with this as vengeance enough, relentlessly pursues his descendants and drowns them if she can. An unusual story of a lake mermaid that was partial to a drink (as was Coomara), is related in the *Sea Enchantress* (1961) by Owen Benwell and Arthur Waugh. The mermaid lived in a small lough near a holy well a few miles from Ennis, and this mermaid had a taste for wine. The butler to the local squire first noticed his master's wine mysteriously vanishing and decided te keep watch and solve the puzzle. The mermaid was caught in the act and the butler seized her and threw her into a cauldron of boiling water. A mass of jelly was all that was left of the poor unfortunate creature. This is as far as the tale goes and no mermaid-style retribution was visited on the butler for his brutal act, although if ever there were a case for vengeance from beyond, then this is it.

The story of blind Maurice Conner and the mermaid is similar in theme to the Cornish tale of the mermaid of Zennor. In the latter a mermaid is enticed from the sea by the beautiful singing of a young man, but in the tale of blind Maurice, it is Maurice's pipe playing that lures the mermaid.

Maighdean-mhara

Maurice was the most wonderful piper in all of Munster and could set any living thing dancing with his playing. One day, as he played at a dance on the sands of Ballinskellig Bay, the creatures of the sea began to tumble out the water and dance there on the beach. The people were amazed, there were crabs and lobsters and fish of every shape and size, and amongst them all, a mermaid danced. The mermaid had long green hair, with the red cohuleen druith perched on top of her head. She made her way up to where Maurice was playing and begged him to come into the sea with her. At first he declined, but finally agreed.

The mermaid led Maurice to the edge of the waves and covered him with a cloak which she also wrapped around herself. A large wave curled over the pair and Maurice was gone, never to be seen again. It is said that seafarers passing the coast of Kerry would often hear music from beneath the waves, and within that music was the unmistakable sound of the pipes of blind Maurice Connor.

Scotland, Orkney & Shetland

The rugged coasts of Scotland are particularly haunted by mermaids, probably more so than anywhere else in the British Isles. In addition to this, Shetland and Orkney, together with the Hebrides, are the strongholds of the seal-folk.

A huge number of tales and legends of water-spirits exist, not just of mermaids and their kin, but of water-horses, water-bulls, and kelpies. Inland they inhabit nearly every Loch and river, offshore; every stretch of coast.

W.Y. Evans Wentz in his *The Fairy Faith in Celtic Countries* (1911), gives the Scottish mermaid the Gaelic name Maighdean-mhara, meaning sea-maiden. Katherine Briggs mentions the Maighdean na tuinne, meaning maiden of the wave, and the curious Highland name 'ceasg' for the same creature. The ceasg was said to have the tail of a grilse (a young salmon) and would grant three wishes if captured, a theme common in mermaid folklore.

The seal-folk were known as the selkies in Shetland and Orkney, and the roane in the Hebrides, especially Skye. 'Roane' is a Gaelic name for the seal, and like the selkie it was believed that the grey seal was really a human in seal form, shape-shifting by means of a special skin. Without their skins the seal-folk were unable to return to the sea, not unlike the magic caps or belts: of the mermaid.

Also in Shetland we come across the sea-trow. A description of the sea-trow by Dr. Samuel Hibbert in *A Description of the Shetland Isles* (1822) is "an animal above the waist, yet terminating in the tail of a fish". Dr. Hibbert also says that the sea-trow resembled a human being of surpassing beauty, had limited supernatural powers and was liable to the accidents of death.

As in other places where mermaid lore is strong, various Scottish families lay claim to ancestry, and according to Benwell and Waugh, belief in Maighdean-mhara was accepted without question as late as the late nineteenth century, especially in the Hebrides, Orkney and Shetland. In his work *Our Highland Folklore Heritage* published in 1926, Alex Polson states that certain people on the west coast of Scotland were known as the 'Sliochd na Maighdear Chriain', 'Children of the Mermaid'.

It was believed that people who were descended from mermaids had special powers, gifts given by the mermaid, and passed down through successive generations of the family. One gift commonly given was protection from drowning at sea, another was skill as a sailor. The two would seem to go hand in hand.

In the first folk-tale we find the common theme of love between a mermaid and a mortal man.

A mermaid once fell in love with a young man of Caithness, and as a token of her love for him the mermaid brought treasure from the deep; gold, silver and jewels to give to the man. Unfortunately the young man was not of an honourable nature, and in turn would often give some of the jewels to young ladies he had taken a fancy to. Often too, he would fail to meet the mermaid when planned, and she began to suspect him and became jealous. One day she met the man at their rendezvous in a wonderful boat, and said that she would take him to a particular cave where she stored all her treasure. The man, greedy for the loot, readily agreed to go with the mermaid. There was treasure in the cave as the mermaid had told, piles of precious stones, gold and silver, but once in the cave the young man fell asleep. He awakened to find that he was bound with golden chains and could only move as far as the mouth of the cave. To this day the youth remains, guarded by the jealous mermaid he had treated so contemptuously.

Another tale of a mermaid imprisoning a man in a cave is the story of Macphie of Colonsay. Macphie eventually escapes, but the mermaid pursues him. Macphie's dog fights the mermaid and both are killed in the terrible battle.

In Scotland we again find the wronged mermaid raising storms to avenge herself and her kin. A mermaid captured accidentally by a fisherman was so incensed that she grabbed his nets and began to tie them in knots. First she tied two knots and the sky grew dark, then she tied a third and a great storm blew up from nowhere. The frightened fisherman managed to persuade the mermaid that her capture had been accidental, and she eventually calmed the storm, allowing the fisherman to get away safely.

Usually, when mermaids were captured by accident, Scottish fishermen had the good sense to throw them back. However, the fishermen would sometimes chance their luck and, on netting a mermaid, would try to strike a bargain before releasing her. Here then we find another common theme in

Scottish mermaid folklore, the granting of wishes by a grateful or captive mermaid.

In *The Peat-Fire Flame* (1937), by Alasdair Alpin McGregor, is the story of a Skye fisherman who demanded three wishes from a mermaid he had taken in his nets. The fisherman got the power to foretell the future, the gift of music and the gift of healing. The mermaid got her freedom. Also from Skye a similar legend; related by Otta Swire in *Skye: The Island and its Legends* (1952). A man once saw a mermaid playing with three baby seals and creeping close he tried to capture the mermaid to obtain three wishes in exchange for her release. The mermaid was alerted to the man's presence, and dived out of his reach, but the baby seals were not so quick and he succeeded in capturing one of them. At that moment the sea seemed to boil and the heads of many mermaids broke the surface. The man nervously held his ground, holding tightly onto the seal, and was addressed by the mermaid he had originally thought to capture. The mermaid demanded that he let the frightened seal go, but the man in turn demanded the mermaid's golden comb before he would do so. The mermaid declined this, knowing that the man would forever have power over her if he owned her comb and offered three wishes instead. The man relented and took the wishes, releasing the seal as the mermaid had asked. In this story the man is first alerted to the mermaid's presence because he hears her beautiful singing voice.

From Cromarty in the north-east comes the tale of *John Reid and the Mermaid*. John Reid was a sailor, and as he walked along the shore one day he heard the beautiful singing voice of a mermaid. He spied the creature sitting on a skerrie, (a reef) near the mouth of a cave, and hoping for three wishes, he managed to creep up and grab the mermaid. The mermaid struggled, but John was a strong man and held her fast. Eventually she gave up the struggle and asked John what his wishes would be. John chose protection from drowning at sea for himself and his friends, good fortune in any venture he might undertake, and a third wish never revealed, save to the mermaid herself. The mermaid granted the wishes, and John released her to the sea. John Reid and his line flourished from that day on.

Mermaids are known for their beautiful singing voices, but in a folk-tale from Girvan, Ayrshire, a serenading mermaid is not appreciated by a local woman. The mermaid in the tale would sit on a particular rock, her favourite perch and sing for hours, all the time combing her long golden hair. The rock was near to the house of Knockdolian and a woman living there had a young baby. The continuous singing of the mermaid, although beautiful, would disturb the sleeping child and the mother ordered her servants to break up the mermaid's rock. This, the woman thought, would rid her of the mermaid, but instead it enraged her, and she uttered a potent curse at the house at the house of Knockdolian and its heirs. A little later the baby was found dead beneath its upturned cradle.

Scotland seems curiously short on mermen, but one strange tale is that of *The Blue Men of the Minch*. The Minch is the channel that separates the mainland from the Outer Hebrides, and the Blue men haunted this stretch of water, particularly the strait between Long Island and the Shiant Islands. The Blue men were blamed for the sudden storms that blew up in the strait, and also for wrecking ships. If a captain could outdo the Blue men at riddles and rhymes he had a chance of saving his ship. The Blue Men were thought to live in underwater caves, but one was captured one day whilst he slept soundly on the surface of the sea. Once on board the Blue man was tied tightly with twine until he couldn't move at all, but not before long two more blue men were seen following the ship. On seeing his companions, and on hearing their voices the captured Blue man broke the twine without effort and dived into the water.

This is a curious legend and no mention is made of the Blue men having fish tails. Donald McKenzie in *Scottish Folk Lore and Folk Life* (1935) gives the theory that the legends concerning the Blue men stem from memories of captured Moorish men marooned in Ireland in the 9th century by the Vikings. These men, known as 'The Blue Moors' were so-called because of the colour of their traditional dress, and were probably slaves of the Norsemen at first, lending an extra element of terror to Viking raids around the Hebrides. The Blue Moors eventually passed into legend as a type of merman.

From the Hebrides we turn to the Orkneys and Shetland, the strongholds of the seal-folk and the sea-trows, but both have their fair share of mermaids.

One tale concerns a Shetland fisherman that once caught a mermaid on his line and in return for her release she gives a warning for the man to "skoom well your fish". The fisherman finds a large pearl in the fish skimmings.

From Shetland comes another more sinister folk-tale, (mentioned in chapter 1). It is the story of a young girl who sees a mermaid washing bloody clothing or the shores of Loch Sin, near Tarbert. Jessie Saxby in 'Shetland Traditional lore' (1876) tells that the girl watched the mermaid as she spread out more than thirty smocks and shirts, all stained with blood, and began to wash them on the grass by the Loch side with a kind of malicious pleasure. This was taken as a bad omen, and sure enough a little later the roof of the local church fell in killing thirty-six people.

The selkies of Shetland and Orkney are the seal-folk, as are the roane in Skye and the Western Isles. On the whole, they are considered to be a far gentler race than their mermaid cousins.

As mentioned in chapter 2, tales of the seal folk are found wherever the Vikings of the early Christian era settled. The mythology of Northern Europe therefore refers to the grey seal, or 'silkie', and as with many mermaid stories, those of the seal-folk are often just variations on a theme. By far the most common sort of tale is the theft of a seal-maiden's magic skin by a mortal man, forcing her to live on land as his wife. A well-known example of this type of tale is told in the Orkney story *The Goodman of Wastness*. The following version of the story is taken from *A Dictionary of British Folktales - Part B: Folk Legends; volume I* by Katherine Briggs.

There was once a wealthy man known locally as 'The Goodman of Wastness', who lived alone on a healthy, thriving farm. Now this man was thought of as a good catch by the local lasses, and more than one sought to marry him and live a comfortable life. But the Goodman had so far rejected all advances, and after a while the rumours began to spread, and the local lasses treated him with contempt, saying that to be intentionally celibate was an unpardonable sin.

The Goodman was not troubled by any of this and continued his single life, enjoying every minute. He would often tell friends that to take a wife would bring nothing but trouble. But things change, and one day the Goodman spied some selkie-folk lying on a flat rock at ebb tide. The creatures were sunning themselves, their magic seal-skins cast about on the rocks nearby. The Goodman contrived to get up close for a better view, and saw the fair-skinned maidens as the most beautiful women he had ever set eyes on. Their unearthly beauty far surpassed that of any human woman he had ever seen before, so the Goodman crept closer still, and came right up to the magic seal-skins lying unguarded on the rock.

Unable to help himself, and quick as a flash, he made a grab for the nearest skin, but at this point the selkie-folk saw him and snatched at their skins in panic. The selkie-folk dived into the sea, but after a while they resurfaced, all appearing as seals now, save one who remained in human form. As they watched, the Goodman turned for home, and still clutching the skin, he set off.

After a while the Goodman heard a pitiful weeping and lamenting behind him. When he turned he saw the selkie-maiden whose skin he had snatched, naked and beautiful, following close behind. The creature was distraught, and when she saw him watching her she began to sob loudly and held out her arms, begging for the return of her skin.

Now the Goodman was so named for his gentle nature, and the sight of the pathetic, sobbing seal-maiden moved him to pity. But the vision of her, beautiful even in her sorrow, aroused another emotion and he fell in love with her there and then. Rather than return her skin, the Goodman persuaded the seal-maiden that it would be no bad thing to be his wife, and left with little choice, she reluctantly agreed.

Time went by and the seal-maiden became a good and loyal wife, caring for her husband well, and bearing him seven children; four boys and three girls. All the children inherited their mother's beauty. But they did not inherit their mother's longing for the sea, and time did not diminish this in her. Although she appeared happy, the longing bore down on her like a great weight. The Goodman, knowing this would happen, had hidden the seal skin well and so the seal-maiden continued to care for him and their children as well as she could.

One day the Goodman and his three eldest lads were away on a fishing trip. The youngest boy and two of the girls had gone out to gather shellfish from the shore, leaving the youngest girl alone with her mother. The seal-maiden set about cleaning the house, and under this pretence, started to search for her skin. She searched and searched, but the skin was nowhere to be found.

Curious, the youngest girl asked her mother what she was doing. The seal-maiden's searching had become more and more frantic, until all pretence of cleaning had gone. She told her daughter that she was searching for an old seal skin that her father had hidden. At this news the young girl exclaimed that if that was all, then she could tell her mother, for she had seen her father hide such a thing in the roof under the aisins.

The seal-maiden gave a cry and rushed to search where her daughter had suggested. After a few moments she pulled the skin triumphantly from its hiding place. Bidding her surprised daughter farewell she rushed from the house and down to the sea. She cried out as she pulled on her seal skin, and her selkie husband surfaced to meet her. The seal-maiden, seal once more, dived into the sea and swam out to him. Together they swam to where the Goodman was fishing with his sons, and the seal-maiden showed her face and called out to him; "Goodman of Wastness, farewel tae thee! I like dee weel do war geud tae me, bit I lo'e better me man o' the sea!"

The seal-maiden dived away and the Goodman never saw her again. Often he would be seen after this, wandering by the shoreline at ebb tide, longing to see his wife again, but he never did.

From Shetland comes a tale in which mermaid and selkie interact.

Against his better judgement, a fisherman once stunned and skinned a seal. The body of the seal was thrown back into the sea, where it recovered. Miserable and cold, the seal swam down to a cave beneath the waves where a mermaid lived, and told her what had happened. The mermaid listened to the wretched creature, and promised to help. The fisherman, meanwhile, had told his companions that he had taken the skin from a dead seal, such was the taboo against killing a seal. The fisherman, however, was becoming remorseful, and all the more so when he and his companions hauled the mermaid up in their nets. The fisherman feared calamity, but his companions decided to keep the mermaid to sell on shore.

The mermaid was laid upon the seal skin, but soon began to expire in the upper air. The mermaid knew what was to become of her, and this was her plan. Her death would release a violent storm and the fishermen would flounder in their boat. The mermaid died soon after and her plan came to fruition. A great storm arose and the fishing boat was wrecked. As the boat sank, the seal's skin drifted down and was swept into the mermaid's cave, where the poor selkie was waiting. Ever after this the selkie folk took it upon themselves to help the mer-folk whenever they could, even at great risk to themselves.

The Wounded Seal-Father is a tale of the seal-folk from the mainland of Scotland. There was once a Caithness fisherman that lived near John O'Groats. This man had killed many seals in his time, as they competed with him for fish. One night, the fisherman met with a man on horseback who wanted to find someone selling seal-skins. The fisherman let the stranger know that he was his man and went with him to a high cliff top where, the stranger said, was someone who would pay well for the skins. At the cliff top the stranger suddenly seized the fisherman and plunged with him over the edge. Down they sank, deeper and deeper into the sea, until the stranger dragged the fisherman, almost dead, into a cave. The fisherman regained his senses, and found to his horror that the cave was full of seals. Worse still, he himself had been turned into a seal. The stranger produced a knife which the fisherman recognised as his own, and it was explained to him that he had wounded the stranger's seal-father with it. Only he that had wounded a seal-father could heal him. The stranger led the fisherman to his wounded seal-father and told the him to place his hand on the wound he had so cruelly inflicted. The seal-father recovered the instant this was done, and the fisherman swore never to harm another seal as long as he lived. The stranger restored the fisherman's human shape and returned him to his home, a lesson well learnt.

Like the seal-folk, the sea-trows have their magical skins. The folk-tale *Gioga and Ollavitinus* is similar in form to the selkie tales where the skin is lost to a man, and its owner is trapped on land.

Fishermen from Papa Stour would often land on the skerries, where the seals basked, and stun them in order to take their skins. One day some fishermen had stunned several seals and skinned them, when a massive swell arose and threatened to trap them on the skerry. They rushed back to their boat, but in their hurry to escape one man was left behind. The swell quickly built up and made it impossible to rescue the trapped man. Eventually his companions had to abandon their rescue attempts, and left the unfortunate man to his fate.

A little later the seals began to return to the rock, and there they saw their skinned companions, who were still alive and coming round. Suddenly several of the seals removed their own skins, revealing themselves to be sea- trows. The skinned seals were also sea-trows, and as the escaping fishermen had left with their skins, they could no longer return to the sea. One of the skinned sea-trows was named Ollavitinus and his mother, Gioga, saw the trapped fisherman and made a deal with him. Gioga said she would carry the man to land if he would return the stolen skins of her son and his companions. The fisherman, thinking he had been left to die, was only too glad to accept the sea-trow's offer. Gioga carried the fisherman through the swell and landed him safely on Papa Stour. The fisherman knew he was lucky to be alive, and was good to his word. He reclaimed the sea-trow skins from his companions, and gave them to Gioga. Ollavitinus was reunited with his mother and they disappeared beneath the waves.

Many Scottish Lochs and rivers are haunted by a particular type of water spirit called 'kelpies'. This is the best known name for the Scottish water-horse, (see chapter 2), and a tale is included here, as kelpies can take on human form. The Kelpie is often involved in the typical 'The Time is Come but not the Man' type story, (a river or other body of water demanding a periodic victim), but the tale *The Water-Horse's Name*, from Otta Swire describes a water-horse in its rarer human form.

A water-horse once asked an old woman and her daughter for food and shelter. Now, the pair did not realise that before them stood the dreaded Each Uisge, as he had changed his form to that of a handsome young man. Before long the older woman grew suspicious because the man's clothing was dripping wet, but nevertheless she bade her daughter invite the man in and feed him. While the man slept off his meal, the mother told her daughter to gently comb through the man s hair, this because all the time her suspicion was growing. The daughter did not question her mother, but did as she was asked. When she had finished she was surprised to find the comb full of shells and sand. Now the mother was sure that they had invited a water-horse into their shieling, and she fled with her daughter. The Each Uisge awoke and gave chase in a fury, changing back to his real, and terrible form as he did.

The Each Uisge soon gained on the pair, and would have had them, but the mother stopped and turned to the supernatural creature at the last second. Then she threatened to shout the name of the Each Uisge "to the four boundaries of the earth". The water-horse stopped in his tracks, so terrified was he at the prospect of his true name being revealed (it made him powerless), and he dived quickly into the burn. Whether the old woman really knew the name of the Each Uisage she did not say, but the threat had saved her life, and that of her daughter. The water-horse still lived in the burn, but certainly never bothered the old woman or her daughter ever again..

Chapter 9

Scandinavia, Denmark and Iceland

In *Scandinavian Folktales* (1988), Dr Jacqueline Simpson says the commonest name for the mermaid in Norwegian, Icelandic and Danish is the *marmennil* with the merman being called the *mermann*. Benwell and Waugh mention also *havfrue* for the mermaid and *havmand* for the merman being used in Norway with *maremind* being used in Denmark. In common with other mermaids, the *havfrue* is a beautiful being, sometimes benevolent and at other times treacherous. Her appearance always heralds a storm. The havmand is quite common in folktales (unlike the British merman) and probably features in as many as his female counterpart. The havmand is usually thought of as benevolent being. The havfruen were thought to have prophetic powers, and if a fisherman should happen to capture a young one (a *marmaeller* - literally 'baby mermaid'), and was brave enough to take it home, it would foretell the future for him.

Scandinavian mer-folk were not necessarily fish-tailed, in fact it is just as common to find them completely human in appearance. The most famous tale fron this general area is, of course, Hans Christian Anderson's *The Little Mermaid* in which we find a slight variation on the theme of a mermaid taking a man for her lover, (she fails in the attempt). Also within the tale is the theme of the mermaid wishing for salvation.

The first tale related here is off at a slight tangent, but nonetheless an interesting one. Legends of the 'Wild Hunt', concerning a spectral huntsman and his hounds, appear all over Northern Europe, including the British Isles. In Denmark it would seem that the hunt's quarry was sometimes a mermaid: *The Green Giant* is taken from J. Simpson's *Scandinavian Folktales* and was originally found in J.M. Thiele's *Danmarks Folkesagn* of 1843.

On the island of Mon is a forest called Gronveld, and here it was that a green giant would hunt every night on horseback. The giant would ride with his head under one arm and his great spear under the other. Farmers would leave a sheaf of corn out for him at night so that he and his hounds would not trample their crops as they passed.

One night the hunting giant stopped at a farm where lived a farmer called Henryk Fyenbo. The farmer nervously came out at the giant's bidding and was told to hold his hounds until he returned. Then the giant rode off and Henryk stood in his doorway, holding the hounds for two hours until the giant returned. When the giant appeared Henryk saw that he had a dead mermaid slung over his horse.

"I've been hunting her for the last seven years," the giant said, "and now, at last I've got her!".

This is an abbreviated version of the tale which goes on to tell how the giant lets Henryk keep the leash with which he held the hounds. While he has it, Henryk becomes a rich man. After he throws the leash away (for some strange reason), he becomes poorer and finally dies quite destitute.

Dr. Simpson also relates a number of other tales, taken from various sources, some of which follow. Scandinavian mermaids were often said to have herds of snow-white cattle. The next tale from Denmark describes this. On the northern coast of Zealand a mermaid would often drive her cattle up out of the sea to graze on the meadows at Tibirke. Now the local farmers did not like her doing this and plotted together to steal the herd from her. One night, once the mermaid and the cattle had come ashore, they drove her and the beasts into a pen and demanded payment from her for the grazing on what they considered to be their land. The mermaid told the farmers that she had no money, and so they next demanded a glittering and costly-looking belt that she wore about her waist. The mermaid had little choice and gave the farmers her belt. The farmers, satisfied with this, freed her and she drove her cattle back down to the beach. But once on the sand the mermaid bade her biggest bull to dig, and at once he began to dig with his great horns. The bull dug so furiously that the sand was swept up and blew inland to cover the fields of Tibirke and it nearly covered the church. The belt had been a costly one indeed, all the more so because when the farmers examined it again they discovered it was made of woven rushes.

Another tale from Denmark concerns a grateful merman giving a fisherman a warning of a storm. In the story the fisherman encounters a merman apparently shivering with cold because he has lost one of his socks, (obviously this is an example of a merman without a fish-tail). The fisherman gives the merman one of his own socks and the grateful merman gives the fisherman a warning of a storm over Norway as a reward. In another version of this story the gift is a glove, and the merman addresses the fisherman as 'glove-friend'.

The Wise Merman is an Icelandic tale and has several versions.

A farmer from Sudurnes lived on a small isolated farm called Vogar, but spent a lot of his time fishing instead of farming. One day he was out fishing, and with his usual heavy haul was something unusual. The unusual thing was a living man tangled in the nets, and the farmer asked him who he was. The man explained that he was in fact a merman and had got tangled in the nets whilst adjusting the cowl on his mother's kitchen chimney. When the merman demanded to be released, the farmer refused point blank, and rowed back to the shore with the now silent merman still on board. Once the boat was beached the farmer's dog ran out to greet his master, and leapt at him so enthusiastically that the farmer grew angry and struck the dog. The merman broke his silence and laughed out loud. The farmer started out across the meadow towards his farm and at one point tripped on a tussock, which he cursed. The merman laughed for a second time. Once at the farm, the farmer's wife greeted him warmly with a hug, and the merman laughed a third time. The farmer was perturbed at the merman's strange outbursts and asked him why he had laughed three times on the journey.

"I won't tell you on any account, unless you promise to take me back to where you caught me," was his reply.

The farmer promised the merman he would do so, and the merman began to explain.

"I laughed the first time when you struck your dog, because he is devoted to you, but you rewarded him with a clout. I laughed the second time when you tripped on that tussock and cursed it, because treasure is buried beneath it. I laughed the third time when your wife greeted you warmly as a lover, but she is unfaithful to you."

The farmer decided to test the merman's word, and thought that the easiest way to do this was to dig beneath the tussock and see if there was treasure there. This he did, and to his surprise unearthed a hoard of gold. The farmer knew then that the merman's word was good and did as he had been asked, releasing the merman at the spot he had captured him. Before he disappeared beneath the waves, the merman thanked the farmer for letting him go and promised him reward would soon be his. Then he was gone.

Not long after this seven grey cows appeared out of the sea and began to graze on the farmer's meadow. The man rushed down to see them, but they were running wild and very nervous. The farmer saw that each cow had a type of bladder on its muzzle, and after he had burst the bladders with a stick the cows became manageable. The farmer realised that these cows must be a gift from the grateful merman.

The cows were fine animals and the farmer prospered for the rest of his life. It is said that the whole of Iceland became populated with the descendants of the sea-cows and are rightly called the 'sea-cow breed' by the people. As for the farmer, he changed the name of his farm from Vogar to Cow's Vogar after the wonderful beasts.

Another version of this story has a much more sinister twist. In this version the third time the merman laughs is not when the farmer greets his unfaithful wife, but when he complains at the quality of a new pair of boots. The farmer is to die three days later. Also the treasure is not found under the tussock, and no sea-cows are involved.

The mermaid is, not surprisingly, well known in the Faeroe Islands, and is said to be beautiful, with long brown hair. Her singing is captivating, but will induce madness in those who listen. Fisherman push their thumbs into their ears if they should hear her. The merman also features in the folklore of the Faeroe Islands. He is a bane to fishermen who will sometimes try to catch him.

A tale taken from William Craigie's *Scandinavian Folklore* (1896) concerns a fisherman named Anfinn, whose lines were always being tangled by a troublesome merman. One day Anfinn succeeded in catching the merman, and took him home. Anfinn kept the merman on the hearthstone in his house, after making the sign of the cross over each of the four corners as a precaution. After a while he started taking the merman on his fishing trips, always being sure to make the sign of the cross over the merman himself before taking him on board. Anfinn's reasoning was good, for the merman would react excitedly, laughing and playing, when a shoal of fish was nearby. Consequently, Anfinn's catches were much improved. If the merman ever dipped his fingers in the sea the shoal was big, and the catch exceptional. But the day came when Anfinn forgot to make the sign of the cross over the merman, busy as he was in some particularly stormy weather. Once far enough out at sea, the merman saw his chance and slipped over the side, free again to plague the local fisherman instead of help them with their catches.

In the tale *Better the Skin than the Child* from Iceland, we have a seal-folk story of the type already described in Scotland.

A man once went to the shore on Midsummer's Eve and saw many naked seal-people lying on the sand, each with a seal-skin lying beside them. The man grabbed one of the skins and when the seal-people fled into the water, one woman was left stranded on the beach. Without her skin she could not change back into a seal and rejoin her own kind. The seal-woman pleaded with the man for her skin, but he refused, saying that she must return to his home and live with him. The seal-woman reluctantly agreed to do so and followed him home.

In time the seal-woman seemed to grow more content with her land life, and behaved as a good wife, taking care of the man's house, and bearing the man's children. The man had locked the seal-woman's skin in an old chest in the smithy and kept the key hidden. Whenever the seal-woman asked him what was in the chest that he always kept so carefully locked, he would say that there was only blacksmith's tools and pieces of scrap metal inside. One day, after several years, the man was away from home, and the seal-woman asked her eldest son where the key to the chest was. The boy answered his mother that he thought his father kept the key with him when he was at home, but hid it in a hole in the wall when he was away. The seal-woman asked the eldest son to search for the key, and he did so.

Eventually, the boy found the key hidden in the smithy wall, and so took it and gave it to his mother. The seal-woman opened the chest, and as she had suspected all along, there inside was her seal-skin. Then she said "Better the skin than the child. The skin never speaks, but a child may talk," and with that she took off for the beach But once on the shore the seal-woman was torn between her children and her longing for the sea and her eldest son, who had followed her, begged her not to leave. But the urge to return to her own people proved too great, and pulling on the seal-skin, she plunged into the sea and disappeared beneath thi waves.

As mentioned in chapter 2, the Scandinavian countries are home to the nokk or nack, a type of solitary supernatural being that frequents rivers, lakes and waterfalls. The nokk in Norway is considered dangerous to man, and is often thought to demand a human drowning once a year. A tale from Norway contains this common motif often associated with river or lake spirits, sometimes called "The hour has come, but not the man". In this tale, a priest hears the nokk's cry from the lake and orders the local people to keep watch for any that may come, wishing to cross the lake, as he knew that the nokk required his yearly victim.

Soon a man appeared at full gallop, and demanded a ferry to cross the lake. The priest refused and urged the man to abandon his journey but the man was adamant that he must cross over. Neither pleas nor threats would dissuade the man, and so the priest ordered the local people, gathered there, to hold him back by force. In the struggle the man was knocked unconscious, and the priest asked someone to fetch water to revive him. No sooner had the water, taken from the lake, passed the man's lips than he died. The nokk had claimed his victim after all.

'The hour has come, but not the man' is associated with many rivers and lakes in England and Scotland. In one case the cry is heard from the sea near Porth Towan in Cornwall, and is thought to be that of a malevolent mermaid demanding a victim. In another, the cry is that of the kelpie of the River Conan in Scotland. One assumes that such tales were originally told to children, and served to teach them to be wary of certain dangerous waters.

Apart from his malevolent side, the nokk or nack is considered a fine musician and will tune a fiddle to perfection if a man leaves it by a stretch of water known to harbour such a being. But there is a catch here also; for the nokk will also leave his own fiddle next to that of the man, and if the man should choose the wrong one the music he plays on it will set the very furniture dancing. In a tale from Sweden a fiddler, who had been taught to play by a nack and was therefore the best around, was asked to play at a party. The fiddler played his best, and started a tune called 'The Nack's Reel'. The people, every one, started to dance whether they wanted to or not, and soon the very furniture joined in. The people were on the verge of dancing themselves to death when a girl arrived late at the party because she had been feeding the animals. Now this girl had a four-leaved clover pinned to her clothes for luck, and it enabled her to see that the nack was sitting behind the distressed fiddler. The girl quickly realised what was happening, and with great presence of mind, stepped forward and cut all the strings on the fiddle, enabling the poor dancers to stop just in time, and getting rid of the evil nack.

Denmark also has its water horses, like the kelpies of Scotland. In one Danish tale, that has variants in Sweden and Scotland, a water-horse that haunted a particular river, persuades several girls to climb up onto its back so they can cross over. The back of the water-horse gets longer as each girl mounts, in order to accommodate them all. Half-way across, one of the girls notices the horse's unusually long back and utters an oath. At her mention of the lord's name, the water-horse vanishes from under them, leaving the girls floundering in the middle of the river. In a Swedish version of this tale the water-horse vanishes at mention of his own name, also known as a protection against the Icelandic water-horse, the 'nykur' or 'ninnir'.

Although the Icelandic nykur is more usually a type of water-horse, it also has human form, and is not unlike the nack or nokk. The nack himself has been known to take the form of a horse in order to lure victims onto his back, he then plunges into the water to drown them. This type of tale is almost identical to those told about the kelpie and Each Uisge of Scotland and the Cabyll Ushtey from the Isle of Man.

Europe and Elsewhere...

Teutonic folklore brings us tales of mermaids and nixes, swan-maidens and the infamous Lorelei of the Rhine. Of the latter mention has already been made; the nature of the Rhine maiden is closely linked to that of the mermaid and the Greek Siren. In *Hero Tales and Legends of the Rhine* (1915) Lewis Spend tells the tale of a Lorelei and Diether, captain of Prince Palatine's guard.

Diether was a captain of the guard in Prince Palatine's army, and it was hi that volunteered to slay the Lorelei that had been responsible for the deathl of the Prince's son. Diether hand picked his companions for the job and after nightfall they made their way to the place where the Lorelei sat. Diether and his men reached the river and saw the Lorelei sitting on her rock, plaiting her long hair in the moonlight. Despite their vow to kill her and hurl her from the rock, they stood bewitched by her beauty and mesmerising song. Thi Lorelei knew that Diether intended to kill her if he could, and so whilst he and his men stood helpless she caused a great storm to arise from the river. The storm took the form of a chariot and three horses in the foam, and in this chariot the Lorelei made her escape. When she had reached mid-stream thei Lorelei sank out of sight and Diether and his men, the spell now broken, realised that they had been thwarted. Their vow of vengeance was never fulfilled.

From Europe comes the romance Melusina or Melusine, a folk-tale of the 'Fair Bride' type. The tale is found in one form or another in various countries including Italy, Estonia, Germany,

Luxembourg and France. Thomas Keightlel recorded a French version in 1850 in his *The Fairy Mythology* and summarised version follows.

Elinas, King of Albania was in mourning for his recently dead wife, and diverted his sorrow by hunting in the forest. One day he stopped at a fountain to drink, and heard the most beautiful singing. Elinas then saw the guardiani of the fountain, the fairy woman Pressina and he fell in love with her at once. Pressina agreed to marry Elinas, but gave him the condition that he must not look upon her at the time of her lying in. Elinas agreed and they were married. In time Pressina bore three daughters in one birth and news was sent to Elinas. The king was overcome with joy at the news and burst into Pressina's bedchamber, thus inadvertently breaking his promise to her. Pressina left Elinas then, taking her daughters with her.

Pressina went to the Lost Island (Cephalonia), a place that could only be found by chance, and she reared her three daughters in peace. The daughters were called Melusina, Melior and Palatina, and when they were fifteen years old Melusina asked her mother about her father. Pressina told her about the breaking of the taboo, and Melusina plotted revenge on her father. With her sisters, Melusina went to the castle of Elinas and imprisoned him inside a mountain. When Melusina told her mother what she and her sisters had done, Pressina was furious and punished Melusina, causing her to become a serpent from the waist down for one day a week.

Melusina wandered the land in search of a husband, and through chance and fate became Queen of the land of Poitou. Melusina became guardian of the Fountain of Thirst, and here she met a hunter called Raymond of Poitou who had stopped for a drink. Raymond fell in love with her instantly, and Melusina agreed to marry him if he promised not to look upon her on a Saturday. After they were married, Melusina had a castle built for them to live in at Lusignan. However, their union was not a happy one, and it seemed as if they were cursed. All their children were born deformed, and Melusina's insistence that Raymond leave her alone on Saturdays started to play on his mind. One day he could stand it no longer and spied on her, locked away in her chamber. It was then that he saw her true form.

Raymond was horrified, not at her appearance, but at what he had done. From her reaction it was obvious that Melusina knew he had spied on her, and Raymond knew he would now lose his beautiful wife forever. Melusina departed, but prophesied before she left that she would haunt the castle of Lusignan, hovering above it as a wailing spectre whenever a current lord of the castle was to die and flying through the air in pain until the Day of Judgement. Melusina became the banshee of Lusignan.

In the French version from Keightly, Melusina has the tail of a serpent, but she is certainly a water-spirit before her transformation to banshee. In a version of the tale from Luxembourg, Melusina is the wife of Count Seigfried, founder of the country. In this version the taboo is the same, but Seigfried is only forbidden to look upon his wife on the first Wednesday of every month, but must keep away for one whole day and one whole night. When he breaks the taboo and spies on Melusina, he sees her sitting in a tub of water with her fish's tail draped over the edge. In this version she is definitely a mermaid, and she leaps out of the window into the River Alzette. She is never seen by Seigfried again, but local people saw a mermaid in the Alzette from time to time.

In Germany a folk-tale set in the Hart forest and called the Water-Maid is another Melusine type story where the wife is most definitely a mermaid. Another mermaid wife from Germany is found in the tale *Brauherd's Mermaid* In this case the husband knows about his wife's 'fishy' nature, but his friends hate and fear her. Brauherd's so-called friends eventually poison the mermaid.

From the wealth of world mermaid folklore come some interesting examples. A Chinese folk-tale tells of a farmer who stole a mermaid's clothes, which she had hung on a tree while she bathed in a well. Without her clothing the mermaid was helpless, and so the farmer forced her to marry him. The mermaid wife bore the farmer two children and remained with him for ten years. She eventually escaped the farmer on a cloud.

This tale shows elements common to European faery folklore, namely that power over the faery is obtained by taking a personal belonging. This bears obvious similarities to the stealing of a selkie skin, or the magic belt or comb of a mermaid. At the end of the tale, the mermaid wife leaves the farmer; faery marriages to humans are doomed to fail in European folklore, and the same would seem to be true in China.

From Indonesia comes a tale of a different kind, concerning a 'Rujung'. A woman once had a miser for a husband, and one day she took a fish from the store to feed her small son. When her husband returned later that day he noticed the fish was missing and flew into a rage. He beat his wife cruelly and she fled from him. Eventually she reached the beach and started to wash the blood off her body. She waded out into the sea and a strange transformation started. From the navel down the woman acquired the tail of a dolphin, and she started to swim about.

Before long her children arrived at the beach, concerned for their mother. When they saw her in the sea they begged her to return home with them, but she could no longer walk on land as she had become a rujung. The woman told her eldest child to collect some of her tears and rub them on their father's back without his knowing. The eldest child did this and the man suddenly saw the error of his ways. He became a loving father from then on, but no matter how hard he searched for his wife he could not find her. In the end the man changed into a porpoise so that he could search the seas, but his wife the Rujung was long gone and he never found her.

In Indonesia there is a belief that dolphins were once women, and the same thing is said of the dugong, (in much the same way as the seal was in Ancient Greece). The dugong is called 'the woman that wears a sad expression and lives in the sea'.

From Japan comes a version of the European Melusine legend called *The Sea-King's Daughter*. The entrance to the sea-king's palace was via a sacred well, guarded by a fearsome dragon. One day a young man peered into the well and was spotted by the sea-king's daughter. She enchanted the man so that he might follow her into her father's palace and there he fell in love with her and they were married. In time the young man longed to see his old home again and made up his mind to go home. The sea-king's daughter begged him not to go, but he remained determined, and so she went with him. The young man built a house for them both on the sea-shore, and after time she became pregnant. The sea-king's daughter made her husband agree not to look upon her until after the baby was born. Of course the man's curiosity got the better of him and he peeped into his wife's chambers. There he saw her in her true form, with a dragon's tail from the waist down. Angry at being betrayed she left with the baby and her husband never saw her or the child again.

Also from Japan is the tale *The Tears of the Samebito*. The Samebito is sometimes described as a black sea monster with green glowing eyes, but more usually he is a type of merman, half human, half shark. The Samebito had been expelled from the ocean by the sea-king, and one day he was confronted by the hero Totaro. Totaro prepared himself, but to his surprise the Samebito did not attack him, and instead asked him for help. Totaro agreed to help and took the Samebito to a lake near his castle where he fed and sheltered it.

Time passed and Totaro fell in love with a beautiful girl called Tamana. Tamana's father was a greedy man and demanded 10,000 precious gems as his bride price. Totaro despaired at the price, and fell gravely ill with worry. Soon it was thought that he was dying. On hearing that his benefactor was close to death, the Samebito began to cry, and his tears turned to jewels where they fell. The Samebito took the tear jewels to Totaro, who realised that there was enough there to pay the bride price. Totaro miraculously recovered there and then, he paid the father, and married Tamana.

Already mentioned in Chapter 1 is the tale of the Amerindian tribe lured into a river by the song of a mermaid. A Christian missionary came to live amongst the Pascagoula people in an attempt to convert them. The Pascagoula lived on the banks of a great river, and worshipped a river goddess with a fish tail, bowing before her image in a temple on the river bank. This concerned the priest greatly, but he persevered and made progress in his work to convert the people.

One night there was a sound of rushing water, and the people saw the river gather itself up into a great column. On the top of the column was their mermaid goddess with her magnetic eyes, her song mesmerizing all who heard it. The people were driven first to ecstasy, then to madness. One by one they followed their goddess and threw themselves into the river. The priest blamed himself for the tragedy, and died of grief. To this day the Pascagoula River is known as the 'Singing River'.

A footnote to this tale is told; If a priest stands on the banks of the Singing River on a night when the moon is at its zenith, and drops a silver crucifix into the water at the place where the mermaid claimed her people, then their souls might be saved. There is a catch however. Any priest who does this to save the souls of the lost Pascagoula tribe will never be seen again. Apparently no-one has tried so far.

From the folk-tales of the Salishan people of British Columbia comes a story called *The Fish-Man*.

Near the mouth of the Fraser River lived a girl that refused all suitors. One night a fish-man came to her and lay with her. The girl asked the fish-man to stay with her until the morning and meet her parents, but he refused. The fish-man came again the next night, and the next, and every night, until the girl finally told her parents.

The girl's parents were angry, but the fish-man caused the sea to recede for many miles, and the village went without fish. The fish-man caused the streams to dry up, and stopped the rain from falling. The people of the village had no water to drink, and no game to hunt because the thirsty animals left the land. The girl told her people that the fish-man had done this because her parents had been angry with him and had wronged him with their harsh words.

The people made a long walk of planks over the mud, right up to the edge of the sea. Then they made a platform, which was covered with mats and blankets. The girl was dressed in her finery, her hair was combed and oiled and her face painted. The people left and the girl sat on the blankets and waited.

The sky became overcast at once, and it started raining. The streams filled again and the sea came in. The little platform with the girl still on it broke free and began to float as the sea rose. The people watched and saw the fish- man appear in the water. He climbed onto the platform and the girl stood up to address the people. She told them that all would be well again, and that she would visit them soon. With that she disappeared into the water with the fish- man.

Two days later the girl returned, and told the people that she now lived with the fish-man in his house beneath the waves. She had brought the people gifts of fish and a promise that they would always be able to catch plenty for themselves. Shortly after this the girl appeared one more time, and brought her new-born baby with her to show the people. Then she dived into the sea and was never seen again.

The above version of *The Fish-Man* is taken from Franz Boas *Folktales of the Salishan and Salaptin Tribes* included in *The Memoirs of the American Folklore Society* Volume 11 (1917). In another version of the same tale, given in *Indian Legends of the Pacific North-West* (1953), by Ella Clark, each time the girl returns from under the sea to speak to her people she is increasingly covered in barnacles. Also, each time she appears she is accompanied by a chill wind.

Chapter 10

Sightings, Cryptozoology and Hoaxes

In 1723 a Royal Commission was set up in Denmark to report on the existence, (or not), of mermaids. The Commission set out to determine whether mermaids were actually real creatures, and during the course of their investigation several commission members had their own sighting.

The Commission members had gone to take evidence in the Faeroes, and were present in a boat which approached a merman who had surfaced off the coast. The merman's gaze apparently unnerved the Commission members so much that they ordered their boat to pull away from him and return to the shore. They later described the merman as having deep set eyes and an intense stare, as well as a long black beard.

This sighting was just as well. If the Commission had decided against the existence of mermaids, the Crown was to have made it illegal to even speak of them. Thankfully no such law was passed.

Today, the term 'cryptozoology' is often used to describe the study, (or theoretical study), of 'hidden nature'. Cryptozoologists search for the mythological creatures, those unrecognised by science. Although mainly creature of folklore, the mermaid makes it... just, into the area of cryptozoological study. Sightings of mermaids and mermen have been reported by seafarers for centuries. Something must be out there!

Alexander the Great allegedly met with mermaids during his travels, "lovely sirens with luring voices". At the shores of the 'Great Eastern Ocean' Alexander encountered the 'Brides of the Ocean' who came ashore at night to dance and sing. Any man who heard their singing went mad. The story surely owes its origins to those of the Ancient Greek sirens.

The Milesians, (who are thought to have originated in Greece), are said to have encountered mermaids who played around their boats as they approached the coast of Ireland. The Milesians would have almost certainly brought mermaid-goddesses with them. Scota, one of their goddesses, (and the name given to the Milesians who eventually settled in Scotland), is probably the same as the Cypriot sea-goddess Scotia according to Robert Graves. By the Middle Ages in Europe, the more affluent nations had taken to sea-faring in earnest. The mermaid was commonly reported, as was her mate the merman.

S. Baring-Gould in his *Curious Myths of the Middle Ages* (1866-8) reported the taking of a merman at Oreford in Suffolk in 1197. The report is well documented and detailed, and tells of a "man-fish" taken in the first year of the reign of King John by fishermen.

The merman was in the shape of a wild or savage man and was presented to a knight, Sir Bartholomew de Glanville, who kept it in his castle at Oreford. The merman was naked and "hairy-bodied", with a long ragged beard. Once detained at the castle he would only eat raw fish and meat, but would not utter a word. One day they took the merman and put him in the sea at the haven, having first placed three ranks of nets across the entrance to prevent him escaping to the open water. But the merman got past the nets easily and dived to the bottom, coming up to show himself now and again, but diving whenever they got close to him. It seemed to the knight's men that the creature was mocking them, but after a while, and to their complete surprise, he seemed to become bored with the sport and came back of his own accord. The merman remained on land for the next two months, but then secretly left and disappeared into the sea for good.

Christopher Columbus reported seeing mermaids on one of his voyages, but told of his disappointment in them! In his work *Purchas His Pilgrimes* (1625) Samuel Purchas recorded that,

"On Friday the fourth of January in the year 1493 (after their account) *sayled from the Port of Nativitie. He saw three mermaids leaping a good height out of the sea, creatures, (he affirmed) not so faire as they are painted..."*

In the 16th century the curious 'sea-bishop' and 'sea-monk', fish with human faces, began to appear. In all probability, the acceptance of such creatures arose from the theory that the sea held a counterpart for every land creature including man. This theory was made very popular in the Middle Ages and was still holding its own into the 18th century.

A sea-bishop was taken in 1531 off the coast of Poland, and described by its captors as a "fish in a bishop's habit". When the strange fish was presented to the king of Poland it expressed its desire to return to the sea, and the king granted its wish. A sea-creature with a human face, cropped hair and a 'monks hood' was taken in 1550. This sea-monk was also to be presented to royalty, but was not so lucky as its Polish cousin, and died en route. The king at Copenhagen ordered that the creature have a Christian burial, as it partly resembled a man.

The 16th and 17th centuries saw many great journeys of discovery. Knowledge of the sciences increased at a remarkable rate, vast new areas of the globe were mapped and scientific explanations for mysterious phenomena were put forward. Belief in mermaids was still fairly commonplace amongst the ordinary people, and reports were still taken seriously. But within academic circles acceptance of such 'impossibilities' was fading.

In 1654, however, a description of a dissected merman was published by the respected Dutch anatomist Thomas Bartholin. The merman was taken, according to Bartholin, off the coast of Brazil, and his dissection drawings showed a "sirene" with a human head and upper body, but a shapeless mass of flesh that tapered towards the end, below the waist. No fins were evident, but Bartholin indicated that he certainly thought the creature to be a type of human adaptation to a marine existence. A drawing of the dissected merman appeared in *Ungenwohnliche Anatomische Geschicte* and bears more than a passing resemblance to an individual with the condition 'Sirenomelia', the 'mermaid syndrome'. This condition is described in more detail at the end of the chapter.

During the 16th and 17th centuries, many renowned and celebrated explorers returned with tales of mermaids and mermen observed at sea. Sir Waiter Raleigh mentions them, as does the great Henry Hudson. Men such as these observed the mer-folk in their natural environment, giving credence to stories of their existence. The academic disbeliever's gave their 'expert' opinions and cast their doubts, mainly from the comfort of dry land. But the mermaids and mermen ignored the so-called experts and continued to appear before astonished sea-farers.

The coastal waters of Sri Lanka have always been known to harbour creatures: half-human, half-fish. In 1560 a report reached England of seven mermen and mermaids being netted off the coast of Mandar. The occurrence was verified by the Physician to the Viceroy of Goa, a man named Bosquez, who actually dissected the seven creatures. Bosquez stated that, both externally and internally, the mermaids and mermen were exactly the same as human beings. His report appeared in *Histoire de la Compagnie de Jesus* no. 276.

Samuel Purchas recorded Christopher Columbus' encounter with mermaids. In *Purchas his Pilgrimes* he also mentions a mermaid "skinne" seen by a traveller: in 1565 at the city of

Thora on the shores of the Red Sea. By the time this mermaid was seen by European eyes, it was, unfortunately, already very old and only the navel, breasts and something resembling a fishes tail remained What happened to the mermaid's head and arms is unknown, but there is every indication that the whole thing was an early fake.

In the year 1608 the explorer Henry Hudson reported a mermaid in his log. Two months after sailing from St. Katherine's Dock, in an attempt to find passage through the North Pole, Hudson records his entry for the 15th of June 1608;

"This morning one of our companie, looking over board, saw a mermaid, and calling up some of the companie to see her, one more came up, and by that time she was come close to the ship's side, looking earnestly on the men"

Hudson goes on to say that from the navel up, her back and breasts were like a woman's, her skin white and her hair long and black, but from the waist down she had the tail of a porpoise, with markings like those of a mackerel. Hudson himself does not claim to have seen the mermaid, but the names of the two men who witnessed her appearance, are given as Thomas Hilles and Robert Rayner. Due to the close proximity of the mermaid, it is unlikely that these men would have mis-identified a seal or a walrus, creatures they would have been familiar with.

Of course, the possibility of hoax exists, as it always does with reports of this nature. Tall tales concocted by bored sailors out of mischief are not entirely unheard of!

The reputation of the mermaid as a dangerous temptress, hungry for the bodies and souls of the drowned, caused a violent reaction when one appeared near Bayonne in 1610. Men grabbed long poles to repulse her, and she uttered a piercing cry before diving back under the water, (from *Legends and Superstitions of Sailors and the Sea*; F. S. Bassett, 1885).

Also in 1610 a mermaid approached some men standing at the harbour-side of St.John's in Newfoundland. A Captain Whitbourne, present at the sighting, described her appearance in some detail. The upper part of the creature appeared as, "...*a beautiful woman, looking cheerful and well proportioned, with hair down to her neck...*" Rather taken aback, the good captain relates that he stepped back from the edge, and the mermaid then dived under the water. At this point he was able to gain a view of her back, which was white and smooth, and from the middle (waist?) down, was shaped like a "..*broad, hooked arrow*". A little later the same creature resurfaced and approached some men in a small boat, (including one of the Captain's servants). Out of fear, one of the men struck the mermaid with an oar and she fell back. She then proceeded to approach other boats in the harbour, causing general fear and panic amongst the occupants.

Captain Whitbourne's description is also included by Samuel Purchas in his *Purchas his Pilgrimes*. Although he, and others, had excellent views of the creature, Captain Whitbourne is careful in drawing his conclusions. He leaves the identity of the creature to his readers, but supposes, "*that such a thing would, in all probability, be called a mermaide*".

Another story from F.S.Bassett's *Legends and Superstitions...* concerns the sighting of a mermaid off the West Indies in 1614. A sea-captain named John Smith reported seeing a creature in the water that resembled a woman from the waist up. She had large eyes, a fine short nose and ears that, according to Captain Smith. were "rather too long". Her hair was green and overall the captain found her attractive. At one point her lower part broke the surface and Captain Smith stated that "*from below the waist the woman gave way to the fish*".

In John Swan's *Speculum Mundi...* (1635), the author theorises on the nature of 'mermaid induced storms'. The tone of Swan's writing leaves us in no doubt that he believed, unconditionally, in the mermaid and her mate. He also believed that the mer-folk were prognosticators of foul weather, rather than the cause.

In 1670 Luke Debes, a Danish clergyman, reported that at Faeroe, westward of Wualboe Eide, many of the local inhabitants saw a mermaid close to the shore. The mermaid stayed in sight for two and a half hours, and had hair so long that it rested on the water, even when she was exposed to the navel. Debes mentions that the mermaid held a fish, head down; interestingly, mermaids are sometimes carved in this pose in churches.

As a holy man, Debes was preoccupied with the resistance of evil, in all its forms, and wrote much on witchcraft and Satan. Debes considered the mermaid as part of this evil, anti-Christian force, and names her as a monster.

Another man who obviously considered the mermaid as a threat was one Mr. Mitten. John Josselyn's *An Account of Two Voyages to New England* (1674) includes a report of a merman seen by Mr. Mitten. The merman placed his hands on the side of the small boat in which Mr. Mitten was travelling and was struck so hard that one hand was severed. The merman fell back into the water which he stained purple with his blood.

Around 1675, Father Louis Nicolas, a Jesuit Priest and missionary to the new Canadian Territories, compiled his zoological work *The Natural History of the West Indies*. In this work Father Nicolas describes the mermen of the Richlieu River. The description is accompanied by a wonderful drawing of a triton-like creature, complete with curving fish-tail, a goatee beard and long hair,

A little later, in 1700, reports reached England of mermaids being captured and eaten by tribes in the Congo. Local folklore described mermaids living in Lake Tanganyika and the River Zaire. The following year, a missionary named Father Francis de Pavia reached Loanga in the kingdom of Matamba. Lake

Matamba, he was told, was the dwelling place of "fish, much like men and women in shape". In the same year, in Slam, Louis le Combe reported on warm-blooded 'fish-women', and a few years later, in 1714 a "bluish-grey marine man" was seen from on board ship by the Superintendent of Churches for the East Indies.

In British waters, a merman was taken near Exeter in 1737. The creature did not fit the typical description of a merman however, and was described as having webbed feet, like those of a duck, as well as the more usual fish's tail. This 'merman' was dragged out the sea in a net, but leapt out and tried to run away. It was knocked down by its captors, and lay on the beach groaning like a human being in pain.

The 18th century seemed to be a popular one for treating mermaids as delicacies. It was not only African tribesmen who were eating them; in 1739 *The Scots Magazine* reported that the crew of the Halifax had killed and eaten mermaids on a journey from the East Indies. The mermaids, it seems, had been taken as they basked on land, and had tasted of veal!

From the end of the 18th century comes a wonderfully detailed description of a merman seen at Havorfordwest in Wales. The sighting occurred in late December 1782, and is told in *A Tour to Milford Haven*, by a Mrs Morgan, the tale having been told to her by an eye witness named Henry Reynolds. Mr. Reynolds was a farmer whose land ran to the cliffs above a bay near Linney Stack.

On the morning in question, Mr. Reynolds saw what he thought was a person bathing in the bay below. Mr. Reynolds was a little surprised, as this was the middle of winter, and he knew the water to be very deep in that part of the bay. The bather looked like a man, and was visible from the waist up, so Mr. Reynolds thought he would move closer and investigate. He actually managed to get within ten yards of the bather, and saw that he was a youth with unusually pale skin.

From his vantage point, Reynolds could now see more detail, and reported these astonishing facts. The youth was upright in the water, visible from the waist. Below the surface was an extremely long tail, like that of a conger eel, continually moving in a circular motion. Mr. Reynolds was now able to determine that, although entirely human from the waist up, the youth had strange features. The arms seemed too short for the body, and were thickset. On the face, the nose ran up between the eyes, and was long and sharp. Instead of hair, a brown ribbon-like substance sprouted from the head and was long enough to reach the water, where it floated about the body.

Mr. Reynolds watched the merman, (he was certain now that this was what it was), as it swam about the bay, apparently washing itself from time to time. In fact Mr. Reynolds watched the merman for about an hour and noted that its movements were rapid, and its look was quite fierce, He finally left to fetch some friends so that they could verify his sighting, but when he returned with others the merman had, predictably, gone.

Meanwhile, in the same year but on the other side of the Atlantic, a merman was seen in Lake Superior by a merchant named Venant Saint-Germain. The merman Saint-Germain claimed to have seen, might more accurately be described as a 'mer-child'. He reported seeing a "small child" with brown skin and short woolly hair rise out of the water. Another witness to this sighting was an old Amerindian woman, who warned that the child's appearance heralded an approaching storm. She described the child as "The God of the Waters and the Lakes". Saint-Germain confirmed that a violent storm did indeed lash the waters of the lake later that evening and lasted three hours.

The sighting on Lake Superior is an interesting one in terms of cultural interpretation. When the strange 'merboy' rose out of the water, the merchant aimed a gun at him. The merchant obviously saw the merboy as a creature of some kind, certainly not a human, and therefore legitimate game, (he traded in furs). He was stopped by the old Amerindian woman who clung onto his arm. She believed that the god of the lake had risen from the waters before them. The old woman predicted that punishment would follow the merchant's transgression: and a short time later a violent storm battered the area. Whatever the pair had witnessed in the Lake, they each saw it according to their own cultural conditioning. Even today the Ojibiwa have legends of the 'Maymaygwayshi' mer-folk with the bodies of children and hairy faces.

Despite the wealth of sightings from around the world, (presumably as sea-faring increased, sightings increased), it was during the 18th century that belief in mermaids, (in Europe at least) began to wane. As the 18th turned to the 19th century, sightings continued but interest at home declined. From time to time mermaid sightings were still reported in the press, but as the 19th century went on, the existence of mermaids was further undermined by a stream of clever (and some not so clever), hoaxes. Despite this fact, the 19th century does turn up some of the best documented and detailed sighting reports.

In the far north of Scotland a schoolmaster from Thurso in Caithness saw a mermaid sitting on a rock. The schoolmaster's name was William Munro and although his sighting actually took place at the very end of the 18th century, it was not published until 1809, and appeared in *The Times*. Mr. Munro reported that he was out walking along the shoreline of Sandside Bay, on fine, clear summer's day. The visibility was excellent, and so when he spotted the mermaid sitting on a rock that jutted out into the sea, he was able later to give a good description. She was naked and sat combing her long, light brown hair. She was slightly on the chubby side, and Mr. Munro reported that her complexion was somewhat ruddy, with bright blue eyes and lips resembling those of a man. Her arms appeared normal in proportion to the body, and his view was so good that Mr. Munro was able to see that her fingers were not webbed.

The schoolmaster watched the mermaid for three to four minutes, before she apparently became aware of him and plunged into the sea. But this was not the last of 'The Caithness Mermaid'. A farmer named John M'Isaac claimed to have seen her in October 1811 at Campbeltown. Mr. M'Isaac described her at having a fish's tail in his report, (William Munro makes no mention of one) It was "a brindled reddish-grey colour and apparently covered with long hair" Mr. M'Isaac also reported that the mermaid spread her tail fin "like a fan" She was entirely human from the waist up, and between four and five feet in total length, but unlike Mr. Munro, Mr. M'Isaac felt that her arms were rather short in proportion to her body. He watched the mermaid sitting on a rock for about two hours, until she pushed herself off and into the sea. Once in the water he was able to get a better view of her facial features, and saw hollow eyes and a short neck.

More witnesses came forward to say that they had seen the same creature. Some boys from nearby Rallinatunie claimed to have seen her on the same day as Mr M'Isaac, and a young girl named Katherine Loynachan reported seeing a creature with long, dark hair, white skin and a brownish fish-tail on rocks near Ballinatunie. Miss Loynachan reported that the creature had the face of a child.

Scotland can boast many more sightings in the 19th century. The rugged Scottish coastline seemed to be as popular as ever with the mer-folk. Already mentioned is the peculiar 'Mermaid of Yell', caught in 1833 and the baby mermaid seen, (and subsequently killed), off Benbecula in 1830. Sixteen years prior to the Benbecula mer-baby, the *Aberdeen Chronicle* reported a merman and mermaid seen by two fishermen off Port Gordon. The merman was spotted first and was described as a tawny colour with grey-green hair. Small eyes were set above a flat nose and wide mouth, and the merman's arms were incredibly long as was the his tapering, scaleless fish tail. The mermaid was not unlike her mate, but the fishermen saw breasts, and reported her hair as being long and straight.

The Mermaid's Rock

Towards the end of the 19th century a long-armed, white-skinned mermaid was seen several times off the coast of Orkney at Deerness. On her final appearance she was shot at, and this was presumably her reason for leaving the area.

In *The Sea Enchantress*, Benwell and Waugh point out that reported descriptions of mermaids seldom conform to those of the beautiful creatures of folklore and legend. Mermaids seen and reported by incredulous witnesses rarely sing, or even talk for that matter. They certainly do not seem to have a predilection for telling fortunes or a tendency to grant wishes, and their appearance rarely seems to herald storms or bad weather. Of course there are always exceptions. A sighting is reported in Peter Buchan's *Annals of Peterhead* in 1819, in which a mermaid appeared to the crew of a ship. A storm blew up and wrecked the ship, drowning all the crew, save one, who told the whole tale to the authorities.

Many sincere witnesses have seen, or certainly believe they have seen, a real, sea-going human creature of some kind. But individuals like the 'Mermaid of Yell' certainly do stretch the point. The creature captured by the Shetland fishermen could hardly be described as human looking. Nevertheless, to the men involved, what they had captured was most definitely a mermaid.

In his *Natural History of Norway* (1755) The Bishop of Bergen, Erik Pontoppidan, describes the sighting of a merman made by three ferrymen of Elseneur. The ferrymen related their experience to the local burgomaster, describing a fish-tailed merman of apparent old age with short curly hair and a neat black beard.

In his book *The Lake Monster Traditions* Michel Meurger points out that the Elseneur sighting sounds very like a description of the traditional artistic representations of Neptune, the Roman sea-god. Meurger argues, (correctly in my view), that sightings of this nature (and there are many), can be ascribed in part as cultural projections. Mermaids and mermen seen holding fish (usually head down) also fit into this category. Mer-folk depicted in church carvings, and in Mediaeval art are often shown in this pose, and the symbolism easily found its way into the descriptions of mer-folk seen at sea.

Pontoppidan was a stout advocate for the existence of the havmand and the havfrau. He also describes baby mermaids, the 'marmaeles'. Regardless of the findings of the Danish Commission only thirty years earlier, by Pontoppidan's time, belief in the mermaid was most certainly on the decline. To have such a distinguished churchman as a supporter must have done the mermaid the world of good. Pontoppidan gathered his information about mermaids with the assistance of other clergymen, and Meurger even states that he could be considered the 'father of cryptozoology'. However the modern 'father of cryptozoology', Bernard Heuvelmans states that Pontoppidan's mer-folk are simply crude descriptions of pinnipeds and sirenians.

Some mermaid sightings can almost certainly be attributed to mis-identification of seals or sirenians (like manatees and dugongs). Glimpsed briefly, at a distance this is understandable, especially if one takes into account the possibility of cultural projection. If a witness believes in mermaids he or she is more likely to see one. Where their tradition is strongest, mermaids are seen more frequently (In the British Isles the majority of 18th and 19th century reports came from Scotland.)

Of course, she does turn up elsewhere from time to time, and sometimes she is obviously something other than a mis-identified seal. In 1881 a mermaid was taken in Aspinwall Bay and exhibited in New Orleans. Examined at close quarters, she was reported on in a Boston newspaper, and described as perfectly resembling a woman from the waist up, with silky blond hair a few inches in length. The arms ended in eagle-like talons instead of hands and the tail below the waist was identical to that of a mullet.

The Aspinwall Bay mermaid had scientists scratching their heads. She was in a perfect state of preservation, and one scientist who examined the corpse stated that "if this can't be a mermaid, because mermaids don't exist, then we give up"

A sophisticated hoax? Hoaxes were certainly popular in the 1800's. Certain types of people will always have an extraordinary predilection for perpetuating elaborate practical jokes, simply for the reward of personal satisfaction. This is as true today as it was in the 19th century.

One such person was the Reverend Robert Hawker, vicar of Morwenstow in Cornwall. The Rev. Hawker was an eccentric chap with a devilish sense of humour, and in July 1825 (or 1826) he decided to impersonate a mermaid. The good vicar made a wig of plaited seaweed, wrapped oilskins around his legs and swam out to a rock a little offshore. Rev. Hawker then sat on the rock, naked from the waist up, holding a mirror and singing.

People walking on the cliff top soon heard him, and caught sight of what appeared to be a mermaid sitting on a rock and admiring herself in a mirror. The news quickly spread to the nearby town of Bude, and from there to the surrounding villages. The vicar kept up the deception on successive nights, and people from all over the area began to congregate on the shore to see if they could glimpse the mermaid. The mermaid would sing for a while each night, and then dive into the sea and apparently disappear. On the last night of the deception, the Reverend Hawker rounded up his singing with a (rather hoarse) rendition of "God Save the Queen", and then disappeared into the sea for good. One is left to imagine the bemused looks on the faces of the onlookers.

Hearing bizarre and mythological creatures became popular in the 19th century although fake mermaids had been exhibited from time to time well before this in sideshows and collections of the bizarre and incredible. The exhibiting of fake mermaids

169

seemed to really take off in the Victorian era and they were reported on in various periodicals of the time.

Composite creations made from the bits and pieces of dead animals, were sewn or fixed together, sometimes quite expertly. Without a doubt, the masters of this art were the Japanese, they excelled at creating the creatures of folklore and mythology. Skilled taxidermists-cum-craftsmen would often go to great lengths to create the perfect specimen. Their hoaxes were often immensely difficult to detect, (at least, before the advent of x-rays and other modern-day tools). Mermaids, it seems, were a speciality, but unlike the beautiful mermaid of legend, the Japanese fakes were usually the upper half of a monkey paired with the tail of a large fish. The Japanese 'sea-monkeys' would appear to be related to the "Mermaid of Yell".

An interesting mermaid was exhibited early in the 18th century. The exhibition was advertised in January 1738, in the *London Daily Post*. The creature had been taken in the waters off Topsham, near Exeter, Devon, and had previously been shown in Exeter, Bristol and Bath. The mermaid was described as having "...regular ribs, breasts, thighs and feet, but had a tail like a dolphin that curled up the back to the shoulders." Apparently the mermaid was not a pretty sight, having a huge mouth full of sharp teeth, a blow hole and a thick neck. Strangest of all was the report of two wings attached at the shoulders.

A transitional mermaid or siren?.... or an elaborate hoax? Strangely enough, a merman was taken in the same waters, a year or so earlier, (described earlier in this chapter). He had the tail of a salmon, but also legs and webbed feet.

A mermaid exhibited in London in 1822 was threatened with dissection to prove its authenticity, but somehow escaped intact. The mermaid had apparently been acquired in China for six thousand dollars by an American gentleman. Understandably he resisted the attempt to carve up his investment.

P.T. Barnum exhibited probably the best known fake mermaid of all time. Barnum's "Greatest Show on Earth" carried the exhibit, nicknamed 'The Fiji Mermaid', along with other marvels and oddities. Despite Barnum's mermaid not being a very good example, it made him a tidy profit. A painting of three beautiful mermaids hung outside the exhibition, and was instrumental in luring the public inside. Not once, did Barnum ever claim that his 'mermaid' bore any resemblance to those in the painting, but as a marketing ploy it worked perfectly.

In 1961 The British Museum mounted an exhibition of fakes. The exhibition included examples from the world of art and literature, as well as other oddities and included two mermaids. The mermaids were thought to have been made in the 1600's and an x-ray examination of one revealed a clever arrangement of wires which held it all together.

One sad footnote to the whole business of fake mermaids is worth a mention here. A rare condition exists in humans, where babies are born with their lower limbs fused together, forming a fleshy 'tail'. The condition is called Sirenomelia, (or sometimes "The Mermaid Syndrome"), and affects 1 in 60,000 pregnancies worldwide. The condition is more common in boys, and especially male identical twins. Sirenomelia is caused when there is a failure of the normal vascular blood supply from the lower aorta in utero.

There is also a suggestion that this condition, (as well as other genetic deformities), is more prevalent in remote, closed communities, where a degree on inbreeding is evident. Midwives were rumoured to sometimes sell the deformed and stillborn infants to travelling sideshows, who would then exhibit them as mermaids, perpetuating the myth. Some of these unfortunates still exist in sideshow exhibits today.

Chapter 11

The Mermaid Today

One does not have to look too far to realise that the mermaid is alive and well in today's modern world. In fact, if you do look, you will realise that her image, the image of the ancient sea-goddess, is all around us. For an ancient, pagan deity she has lasted well. In her raw elemental form she is used to represent water; more than this, she represents the union of the human spirit with the life-giving waters from whence it came.

I said at the beginning of this book that there are three ways of approaching the study of mermaids. One is the belief in her as the semi-human, water-fairy, a creature of folklore. Benwell and Waugh, writing in 1961, point out that it was impossible to say that belief in her had been utterly extinguished. Nearly forty years on this statement still holds true. It has been suggested earlier that in remote areas with a strong historical tradition of the mer-folk and other sea-spirits, belief in her probably still lingers. Further to this, belief in fairies today is generally more widespread than most people realise, especially if we include the idea of fairies as nature elementals, in which the mermaid may be included to represent the element of water. As the water-fay, undine or mermaid she may be invoked in elemental magic as the guardian of the west.

Elsewhere in the world we find evidence for the belief in mermaids as real creatures. In Java reverence is still paid to the mermaid goddess Loro Kidul. Kings of Java would wade out into the waves to ask for her guidance in matters of an important nature. A large proportion of modern Javanese are Muslim, but still offer respect to the greatest of their ancient goddesses. Offerings are left to Loro Kidul on the beach, or at beach-side temples. In nearby Bali the merman-god Waruna is still worshipped and offerings are made to him in a similar way.

In Africa mermaids are still believed to haunt various rivers and lakes, as well as the sea. The same is true in Canada and america amongst certain tribes. The New Mexico desert is an odd place to find mermaids, but along the San Juan River (especially in the region of the Navajo Lake), there are many legends about her and ancient petroglyphs depicting her are found high on the canyon walls.

Mermaid sightings are rarer these days, but are sometimes reported, (I suspect that there are some that go unreported for fear of ridicule). At the turn of the century, one Alexander Gunn saw a mermaid at a range of only a few feet, as she lay on a rock ledge waiting for the tide to come in. Mr. Gunn described her look to be 'both frightened and angry'. In Scotland in 1939 a mermaid was seen by a woman fishing from a boat. The mermaid had a beautiful face, golden hair, blue eyes and a delicate complexion. The woman's ghillie informed her that local people knew of the mermaid and thought she was 'uncanny'. In 1947 a fisherman saw a mermaid on the Isle of Muck. She was about twenty yards offshore, sitting on a floating herring box that was used to keep lobsters. The mermaid was combing her hair, but dived out of sight as soon as she realised she was being watched.

In 1957 a mermaid apparently came aboard the raft Tahiti-Nui. The Tahiti-Nui was a raft constructed to a traditional plan, and built by the late Eric de Bisschop to prove that ancient Polynesians could have made it across the sea to Chile, (the reverse of the more famous Kon-Tiki journey in the early 50's). The mermaid was seen by a sailor on night watch, who thought, at first, that he was looking at a dolphin. The creature had jumped aboard the raft and stood upright on its tail. When confronted it knocked the terrified man down. The mermaid was described as being 'smelly' and having fine 'seaweed like' hair. After being knocked over by the mermaid the sailor was left with silvery fish-scales all over his arms. Mermaid or not, whatever the apparition had been, it certainly preceded a spell of bad luck and tragedy for de Bisschop. The Tahiti-Nui did not complete the journey to Chile, but floundered within sight of its goal. Eric de Bisschop constructed a second raft in Chile for a return journey, but this one was wrecked in the Cook Islands and de Bisschop died of injuries he received.

Reported sightings in recent years are almost unheard of, although the mermaid does occasionally pop her head above the surface to bemuse and confound the odd witness. A mermaid was seen and reported as recently as 1991 by a security guard off the coast of Queensland, Australia. But on the whole she (sensibly?) seems to be keeping herself to herself. Perhaps the huge increase in shipping, and the pollution that inevitably accompanies it is to blame. No doubt mermaid numbers are in decline, along with many of the other species which share their realm. No-one has yet reported a mermaid washed up dead and covered in oil, but perhaps it is only a matter of time!

She may be rare in her natural habitat, but she is as popular as ever (if not more so) in the minds of certain sections of the population. The mermaid is frequently painted by fantasy artists, and is a popular subject in tattooing. Photographers have used the technology now available to them to create stunning and, more often than not, erotic images of her. It would seem that the mermaid cannot escape her age-old association with sex, the Church's conditioning goes too deep for that, but that sexual imagery can now be viewed in a more positive way. On the whole artists and photographers are depicting the beauty and wildness of the erotic, and the mermaid's new PR has created a far better image for her than that perpetuated by the mediaeval Church.

A number of films have been made about mermaids. Aside from the 1989 Disney animation of *The Little Mermaid* there is the 1984 film *Splash*, starring Darryl Hannah as the mermaid Madison. In order to pursue a man she has fallen in love with,

Madison acquires legs so she can move on land. To start with Madison cannot speak, but learns later. In the 1948 film *Mr.Peabody's Mermaid* the mermaid, played by Anne Blyth, cannot speak but sings beautifully. *Mr.Peabody's Mermaid* is based on a story by Guy and Constance Jones. In *The Little Mermaid*, the mermaid in question bargains with a sea- witch and swaps tail for legs in order to come on land and win the heart of a human lover. But the cost is high and the witch keeps the mermaid's voice. In the Hans Anderson tale the mermaid also endures agonies when she walks on land. Possibly due to the popularity of the Disney version, a completely live action version of *The Little Mermaid* is currently in production.

The Disney animation has almost single-handedly reintroduced the mermaid to a younger audience. The spin-off merchandising from the film has produced mermaid dolls and other items bearing her image, (even a young child's potty!)

The original 'Little Mermaid' is, of course, commemorated by the famous statue by Edvard Erikson in Copenhagen. A wonderful representation, she sits curled very naturally on a rock in the Sound. Erikson was inspired to create his statue of her after seeing a ballet version of Anderson's tale at The Royal Theatre in Copenhagen. He used his young wife as his model. The statue was purchased by one Carl Jacobson via the New Carlsberg Foundation, which had been set up for the 'furtherance of art'. It was Jacobson who was inspired to place the mermaid in the Sound in 1913, where she still sits today to be admired by thousands of visitors to the city. However not all, it seems, admire the statue and she has been beheaded twice. The first time was in 1964 and the head was never found, but a replacement head was cast from the original mould. Over the years she has attracted graffiti and lost an arm in 1983.

The most recent beheading was on the 6th January 1998, and a group calling themselves the 'Radical Feminist Faction' claimed responsibility. The group said the mermaid represented a

Wooden mermaid carving (modern Balinese)

symbol of hostility to women and the sexually obsessed dreams of men in which a woman was only a body with no head. The group retracted their claim on the 8th of January and the next day the head was left in a box outside a television studio 12 miles from the capital. The mermaid was restored the following month, and a man was subsequently arrested and charged with vandalism.

Another mermaid statue, less well known perhaps, is situated on the banks of The Vistula in Warsaw (a river noted for its legends of resident mermaids). The mermaid of Warsaw has been represented since the middle of the 18th century on the city's coat of arms. In both the statue and the coat of arms she is shown with a sword held aloft, and a shield on her arm. The mermaid is the protector of the city, and was taken to the hearts of the Warsaw people in World War II, who used her as a symbol of resistance against the Nazi invaders. The Polish Resistance would draw her image on the walls around the city, knowing that, if caught, they would be executed.

Today the symbolism of the mermaid has not gone unnoticed by the advertising agencies. A recent television advertisement for a popular brand of jeans shows a sailor being swept into the sea, and sinking into the depths, where he is approached by three mermaids. The man is wearing the jeans in question, and the mermaids make vigorous attempts to remove them, (the sexual association being fairly blatant in this case). One of the mermaids kisses the man, but the superior fit of the sailor's jeans thwarts their attempts to remove them. The sailor then makes good his escape with his virtue left intact! Interestingly enough the advertisement was deemed too steamy for American television, and consequently was not shown there.

Apart from her very appearance as a semi naked woman, (albeit with fish-tail), the sexual theme is not always pursued. A French advertisement for IBM computers shows a mermaid using a laptop PC to type up the songs she uses to lure seafarers to their doom. A well known fast-food chain has used mermaid imagery to sell their hamburgers; she has been used to promote a French designer perfume, and in a strange twist, a mermaid was once used to advertise a particular make of shoes!

Today, an excellent hunting ground for the mermaid is on the internet. Many sites are devoted mainly to Disney's *Little Mermaid*, but plenty have been set up by 'merphiles' that are devoted to mermaids and all things associated with them. Many of the sites have been gathered together in an indexed collective, called 'The Mermaid Net' (52 web sites at time of writing). The web sites display artwork, poetry and even short stories. There is mythology, folklore and sightings. References are listed for further reading, mermaid related items are offered for sale. She is generally celebrated in all her forms. One web site, 'Seatails Online', claims to be one of the first, and one of the largest devoted to mermaids. The site is the internet version of a U.S. magazine, devoted to the mer-folk, called 'Seatails'.

From ancient and powerful, life-giving and life-taking sea-goddesses, through the water-spirits from a multitude of cultures, to Disney's quaint fish-tailed heroine 'Aerial', the mermaid has come a long way. And all this despite the Church's attempts to discredit her. The fact remains that of all the ancient goddesses, her image is one of the most enduring. The mermaid will continue to swim through the seas and oceans of the world and through the imaginations of human-kind as long as there is a need for her to do so.

She symbolises the primeval waters, the womb of the world, from whence we all came and inevitably must return. We cannot escape her, for she created us and lives within us all. We cannot survive without her

Long may our need for her continue.

Bibliography

Aarne, Antti (revised by Stith Thompson) - *Types of the Folktale* (1910)

Aldovardi, Ulysses - *Historia Monstrorum* (1599)

Baring-Gould, S - *Curious Myths of the Middle Ages* (1866-8)

Bassett, F.S. - *Legends and Superstitions of Sailors and the Sea* (1885)

Benwell, Gwen & Waugh, Arthur - *The Sea Enchantress* (1961)

Boaz, Franz - *Folk-Tales of the Salishan and Sataptin Tribes* (1917)

Bottrell, William - Traditions and Hearthside Stories of West Cornwall (1870)

Briggs, Katherine - *A Dictionary of Fairies* (1976)

Briggs, Katherine - *A Dictionary of British Folktales in the English Language* part b (1970)

Broome, Dora - *Fairy Tales from the Isle of Man* (1951)

Buchan, Peter - *Annals of Peterhead* (1819)

Burne, C.S. and Jackson, G.F. - *Shropshire Folk-lore* (1883)

Child, F.J. - *English and Scottish Popular Ballads* (1890)

Clark, Ella - *Indian Legends of the Pacific North-West* (1953)

Courtney, Margaret - *Cornish Feast and Folklore* (1890)

Craigie, William - *Scandinavian Folklore* (1896) Crofton

Croker, Thomas - *Fairy Legends and Traditions of the South of Ireland* (1825)

Cromek, R.H. - *Remains of Nithsdale and Galloway Song* (1810)

Crossing, William - *Folklore and Legends of Dartmoor* (1914)

Dash, Mike - *Borderlands* (1997)

Dennison, W.T. - *Orcadian Sketchbook* (1880)

Evan-Wentz, W.Y. - *The Fairy Faith in Celtic Countries* (1911)

Farrar, Janet and Stewart - *The Witches Goddess* (1987)

Farrar, Janet and Stewart - *The Witches God* (1989)

Fox, Matthew - *The Coming of the Cosmic Christ* (1988)

Gayarre, Charles - *History of Louisiana* (1883)

Gill, Walter - *A Manx Scrapbook* (1929)

Gill, Walter - *A Second Manx Scrapbook* (1932)

Graves, Robert - *The White Goddess* (1961)

Hamilton, Robert - *History of Whales and Seals* (1839)

Hartland, E.S. - *The Science of Fairy Tales* (1891)

Henderson, William - *Folklore of the Northern Counties* (1879)

Hibbert, Samuel - *Description of the Shetland Isles* (1822)

Hunt, Robert - *Popular Romances of the West of England* (1881)

179

Jones, William - *Credualities, Past and Present* (1880)
Josselyn, John - *An Account of Two Voyages to New England* (1674)
Keightly, Thomas - *The Fairy Mythology* (1850)
Knappert, Jan - *African Mythology* (1990)
Knappert, Jan - *Pacific Mythology* (1992)
Leather, E.M. - *Folk-lore of Herefordshire* (1912)
Macculloch, J.A. - *Myths of all Races: Celtic* (1918)
Machal, Ian - *Myths of all Races: Slavic* (1918)
Mackenzie, Donald - *Scottish Folk Lore and Folk Life* (1935)
Markale, Jean - *Women of the Celts* (1975)
McGregor, Alasdair Alpin - *The Peat-Fire Flame* (1937)
Meuger, Michel - *Lake Monster Tradition* (1988)
Nicolas, Father Louis - *The Natural History of the West Indies* (1675)
Polson, Alex - *Our Highland Folk-lore Heritage* (1926)
Pontoppidan, Bishop Erik - *The Natural History of Norway* (1755)
Purchas, Samuel - *Purchas His Pilgrimes* (1625)
Rhys, Sir John - *Celtic Folk-Lore vol 1* (1901)
Saxby, Jesse - *Shetland Traditional Lore* (1876)
Seltman, Charles - *The Twelve Olympians* (1952)
Sikes, Wirt - *British Goblins* (1880)
Simpson, Jacqueline - *Scandinavian Folk-Tales* (1988)
Spence, Lewis - *Hero Tales and Legends of the Rhine* (1915)
Swan, John - *Speculum Mundi, or A Glasse representing the Face of the World* (1635)
Swire, Otta - *Skye: The Island and its Legends* (1952)
Thiele, J.M. - *Danmarks Folkesagn* (1843)
Thomson, David - *The People of the Sea* (1954)
Waldron, George - *Description of the Isle of Man* (1744)
Werner. E.T.C. - *Myths and Legends of China* (1933)

Index

Handbook of Fairies　by Ronan Coghlan

This is a detailed guide to fairies and other otherworldly beings. The different types of fairy and other otherworld beings are described, together with stories and legends about them. The possible origins of fairies are also discussed as are various theories about them, their links or differences from aliens, the passing of time in the Otherworld and other fascinating topics. When we consider the realm of Faerie, we should hesitate to attribute it to the mere superstition of our ancestors, on whom we are encouraged to shower unmerited contempt by a world-view which tells us we are constantly making what it terms "progress". Features marvellous illustrations by Marc Potts. ISBN 186163 042 5　£9.95

Wondrous Land - The Faery Faith of Ireland　by Kay Mullin

"....a delight...a living, personal story from the Atlantic edge..." 3rd Stone
Dr Kay Mullin, a clinical psychologist by profession, was introduced to the world of faery by spirit channelled through a medium. That meeting led to extensive research in Ireland, collecting stories both old and new - from people who not only know of faeries, but see them too - in the land so long associated with them. The result is this wonderful book. The faery faith is real, alive and growing in Ireland. Illustrated by Cormac Figgis. ISBN 186163 010 7　£10.95

Real Fairies　by David Tame　*"Here we have first-hand accounts....reliable witnesses...Highly recommended!"* The Cauldron Encounters with fairies seem to be increasing. This book relates the experiences of many people, some famous (such as BBC presenter Valerie Singleton), some clairvoyant, some everyday, who have seen and met members of the fairy kingdom. It appears that our world and theirs are drawing closer together again and it is possible for more and more people to see what we have been told by some for generations does not exist. ISBN 186163 0719　£9.95

The Fairies in the Irish Tradition　by Molly Gowen A comprehensive study of the fairy nature and its manifestations in the Irish tradition, illustrated with stories and legends and illuminated with superb artwork. Contents include: Fairy Nature - fallen angels, elementals and ghosts; Fairies in the Landscape; The Banshee; History of the Sidhe; the Fairy Doctor; Tir na nOg; magical animals, the Pooka, the King of Cats and Demon Dogs. Many superb illustrations by Lavinia Hamer. ISBN 186163 0859 £7.95

Fairy Lore　by Anna Franklin and Paul Mason There are legends of fairies all over the world, mysterious creatures who live apart from the race of mankind, but who are sometimes seen in wild and lonely places. The authors explore the world of the fairies - what they look like; the fairy realms such as Hy-Breasail, Lochlann, Ynis Gwyddrin and Emani Ablch; fairy food, protection against fairies and their ills; fairy plants and animals, fairy days and festivals, visits to fairyland, fairy loves and their links with magic. They also investigate what fairies are - fallen angels, a separate race, ancestor cult, nature spirits, old gods, UFOs, hallucinations, shamanic experience etc. A beautiful book to own and a real must for anyone with even a passing interest in fairies. Beautifully and extensively illustrated with a blend of traditional pictures and original artwork by Paul Mason. ISBN 186163 1073　£10.95

FREE DETAILED CATALOGUE

Capall Bann is owned and run by people actively involved in many of the areas in which we publish. A detailed illustrated catalogue is available on request, SAE or International Postal Coupon appreciated. **Titles can be ordered direct from Capall Bann, post free in the UK** (cheque or PO with order) or from good bookshops and specialist outlets.

Do contact us for details on the latest releases at: **Capall Bann Publishing, Freshfields, Chieveley, Berks, RG20 8TF.** Titles include:

A Breath Behind Time, Terri Hector
Angels and Goddesses - Celtic Christianity & Paganism, M. Howard
Arthur - The Legend Unveiled, C Johnson & E Lung
Astrology The Inner Eye - A Guide in Everyday Language, E Smith
Auguries and Omens - The Magical Lore of Birds, Yvonne Aburrow
Asyniur - Womens Mysteries in the Northern Tradition, S McGrath
Beginnings - Geomancy, Builder's Rites & Electional Astrology in the
        European Tradition, Nigel Pennick
Between Earth and Sky, Julia Day
Book of the Veil , Peter Paddon
Caer Sidhe - Celtic Astrology and Astronomy, Vol 1, Michael Bayley
Caer Sidhe - Celtic Astrology and Astronomy, Vol 2 M Bayley
Call of the Horned Piper, Nigel Jackson
Cat's Company, Ann Walker
Celtic Faery Shamanism, Catrin James
Celtic Faery Shamanism - The Wisdom of the Otherworld, Catrin James
Celtic Lore & Druidic Ritual, Rhiannon Ryall
Celtic Sacrifice - Pre Christian Ritual & Religion, Marion Pearce
Celtic Saints and the Glastonbury Zodiac, Mary Caine
Circle and the Square, Jack Gale
Compleat Vampyre - The Vampyre Shaman, Nigel Jackson
Creating Form From the Mist - The Wisdom of Women in Celtic Myth and
        Culture, Lynne Sinclair-Wood
Crystal Clear - A Guide to Quartz Crystal, Jennifer Dent
Crystal Doorways, Simon & Sue Lilly
Crossing the Borderlines - Guising, Masking & Ritual Animal Disguise in the
        European Tradition, Nigel Pennick
Dragons of the West, Nigel Pennick
Earth Dance - A Year of Pagan Rituals, Jan Brodie
Earth Harmony - Places of Power, Holiness & Healing, Nigel Pennick
Earth Magic, Margaret McArthur

189

Eildon Tree (The) Romany Language & Lore, Michael Hoadley
Enchanted Forest - The Magical Lore of Trees, Yvonne Aburrow
Eternal Priestess, Sage Weston
Eternally Yours Faithfully, Roy Radford & Evelyn Gregory
Everything You Always Wanted To Know About Your Body, But So Far
    Nobody's Been Able To Tell You, Chris Thomas & D Baker
Face of the Deep - Healing Body & Soul, Penny Allen
Fairies in the Irish Tradition, Molly Gowen
Familiars - Animal Powers of Britain, Anna Franklin
Fool's First Steps, (The) Chris Thomas
Forest Paths - Tree Divination, Brian Harrison, Ill. S. Rouse
From Past to Future Life, Dr Roger Webber
Gardening For Wildlife Ron Wilson
God Year, The, Nigel Pennick & Helen Field
Goddess on the Cross, Dr George Young
Goddess Year, The, Nigel Pennick & Helen Field
Goddesses, Guardians & Groves, Jack Gale
Handbook For Pagan Healers, Liz Joan
Handbook of Fairies, Ronan Coghlan
Healing Book, The, Chris Thomas and Diane Baker
Healing Homes, Jennifer Dent
Healing Journeys, Paul Williamson
Healing Stones, Sue Philips
Herb Craft - Shamanic & Ritual Use of Herbs, Lavender & Franklin
Hidden Heritage - Exploring Ancient Essex, Terry Johnson
Hub of the Wheel, Skytoucher
In Search of Herne the Hunter, Eric Fitch
Inner Celtia, Alan Richardson & David Annwn
Inner Mysteries of the Goths, Nigel Pennick
Inner Space Workbook - Develop Thru Tarot, C Summers & J Vayne
Intuitive Journey, Ann Walker Isis - African Queen, Akkadia Ford
Journey Home, The, Chris Thomas
Kecks, Keddles & Kesh - Celtic Lang & The Cog Almanac, Bayley
Language of the Psycards, Berenice
Legend of Robin Hood, The, Richard Rutherford-Moore
Lid Off the Cauldron, Patricia Crowther
Light From the Shadows - Modern Traditional Witchcraft, Gwyn
Living Tarot, Ann Walker
Lore of the Sacred Horse, Marion Davies
Lost Lands & Sunken Cities (2nd ed.), Nigel Pennick
Magic of Herbs - A Complete Home Herbal, Rhiannon Ryall
Magical Guardians - Exploring the Spirit and Nature of Trees, Philip Heselton
Magical History of the Horse, Janet Farrar & Virginia Russell
Magical Lore of Animals, Yvonne Aburrow
Magical Lore of Cats, Marion Davies
Magical Lore of Herbs, Marion Davies

190

Magick Without Peers, Ariadne Rainbird & David Rankine
Masks of Misrule - Horned God & His Cult in Europe, Nigel Jackson
Medicine For The Coming Age, Lisa Sand MD
Medium Rare - Reminiscences of a Clairvoyant, Muriel Renard
Menopausal Woman on the Run, Jaki da Costa
Mind Massage - 60 Creative Visualisations, Marlene Maundrill
Mirrors of Magic - Evoking the Spirit of the Dewponds, P Heselton
Moon Mysteries, Jan Brodie
Mysteries of the Runes, Michael Howard
Mystic Life of Animals, Ann Walker
New Celtic Oracle The, Nigel Pennick & Nigel Jackson
Oracle of Geomancy, Nigel Pennick
Pagan Feasts - Seasonal Food for the 8 Festivals, Franklin & Phillips
Patchwork of Magic - Living in a Pagan World, Julia Day
Pathworking - A Practical Book of Guided Meditations, Pete Jennings
Personal Power, Anna Franklin
Pickingill Papers - The Origins of Gardnerian Wicca, Bill Liddell
Pillars of Tubal Cain, Nigel Jackson
Places of Pilgrimage and Healing, Adrian Cooper
Practical Divining, Richard Foord
Practical Meditation, Steve Hounsome
Practical Spirituality, Steve Hounsome
Psychic Self Defence - Real Solutions, Jan Brodie
Real Fairies, David Tame
Reality - How It Works & Why It Mostly Doesn't, Rik Dent
Romany Tapestry, Michael Houghton
Runic Astrology, Nigel Pennick
Sacred Animals, Gordon MacLellan
Sacred Celtic Animals, Marion Davies, Ill. Simon Rouse
Sacred Dorset - On the Path of the Dragon, Peter Knight
Sacred Grove - The Mysteries of the Forest, Yvonne Aburrow
Sacred Geometry, Nigel Pennick
Sacred Nature, Ancient Wisdom & Modern Meanings, A Cooper
Sacred Ring - Pagan Origins of British Folk Festivals, M. Howard
Season of Sorcery - On Becoming a Wisewoman, Poppy Palin
Seasonal Magic - Diary of a Village Witch, Paddy Slade
Secret Places of the Goddess, Philip Heselton
Secret Signs & Sigils, Nigel Pennick
Self Enlightenment, Mayan O'Brien
Spirits of the Air, Jaq D Hawkins
Spirits of the Earth, Jaq D Hawkins
Spirits of the Earth, Jaq D Hawkins
Stony Gaze, Investigating Celtic Heads John Billingsley
Stumbling Through the Undergrowth , Mark Kirwan-Heyhoe
Subterranean Kingdom, The, revised 2nd ed, Nigel Pennick
Symbols of Ancient Gods, Rhiannon Ryall

Talking to the Earth, Gordon MacLellan
Taming the Wolf - Full Moon Meditations, Steve Hounsome
Teachings of the Wisewomen, Rhiannon Ryall
The Other Kingdoms Speak, Helena Hawley
Tree: Essence of Healing, Simon & Sue Lilly
Tree: Essence, Spirit & Teacher, Simon & Sue Lilly
Through the Veil, Peter Paddon
Torch and the Spear, Patrick Regan
Understanding Chaos Magic, Jaq D Hawkins
Vortex - The End of History, Mary Russell
Warp and Weft - In Search of the I-Ching, William de Fancourt
Warriors at the Edge of Time, Jan Fry
Water Witches, Tony Steele
Way of the Magus, Michael Howard
Weaving a Web of Magic, Rhiannon Ryall
West Country Wicca, Rhiannon Ryall
Wildwitch - The Craft of the Natural Psychic, Poppy Palin
Wildwood King , Philip Kane
Witches of Oz, Matthew & Julia Philips
Wondrous Land - The Faery Faith of Ireland by Dr Kay Mullin
Working With the Merlin, Geoff Hughes
Your Talking Pet, Ann Walker

FREE detailed catalogue and FREE 'Inspiration' magazine

Contact: Capall Bann Publishing, Freshfields, Chieveley, Berks, RG20 8TF